The Indwelling Spirit of Christ

Finding Life in His Presence

RON HEINECKE

THE INDWELLING SPIRIT OF CHRIST

Finding Life in His Presence

Cover design and typography by Nathan Sewell

ISBN-13: 978-1547177769
ISBN-10: 1547177764

DEDICATION

To my ever-present indwelling Lord and Savior Jesus Christ, and to my wonderful wife, Rita, who is God's demonstration of His superabundant grace to me.

ACKNOWLEDGEMENTS

Special thanks to Sandi Tompkins and our Garden Valley Writers Group for their patient help in rewriting and editing this book.

Table of Contents

PREFACE

On a typical gravestone, there is a date of birth, date of death, and a dash between these dates representing one's life. The vital thing is fully experiencing life, the indwelling life of Christ to be specific.

Christians often focus on the date we were "born again" and the day we will be with Jesus in Heaven, neglecting life with Jesus now. We pray for Jesus to be manifested at His second coming, but the apostle Paul also prayed the "life of Jesus would be manifested in our mortal bodies" (2 Corinthians 4:10–11). "For of His fullness we have all received" (John 1:16).

A woman's doctor told her she was dying. Sobbing she said, "I am not crying because I am dying. I am crying because I have never really lived." Sadly many Christians seldom rest in the peace and joy of the indwelling life of God, the fruit of God's Spirit. Christ *is* our life (Colossians 3:4). His work on the cross is a finished work. His work within us is ongoing, for He said He'd never leave us.

A pastor in Africa was asked the reason for the continuing revival in his church. He simply said, "Living with Jesus in the *now*." This means focusing on an ever-present indwelling Savior, not an experience we once had, or a Heaven we will one day possess.

The message of Jesus we will examine begins in John 14 at the Last Supper, just after Judas left to betray Jesus, concluding at the end of John 17, where Jesus prays we will be perfected by unity with Him. Previously Jesus said we must be perfect. Now He introduces the New Covenant, the way of perfection—living by the life of our very significant Other – our indwelling Lord.

> *Jesus' death and resurrection made us fit for Heaven.*
>
> *His indwelling Holy Spirit makes us fit for Earth.*
>
> *He substituted for us in His death. He substitutes in us as our life.*

PART I

1. THE TIME OF OUR VISITATION

For the days will come upon you when your enemies...will not leave in you [Jerusalem] one stone upon another, because you did not recognize the time of your visitation (Luke 19:43–44).

The Jews of Jesus' day looked for a physical king to rule a physical kingdom and missed their Messiah. Christians today are looking forward to the second physical coming of our Messiah and often sadly miss His presence with us here on Earth. "In Him was life, and the life was the Light of men. The Light shines in the darkness, and the darkness did not comprehend it" (John 1:4–5).

Jesus prophesied judgment on the people of Israel because He, their Messiah, whom more than fifty Old Testament prophecies foretold, stood before them, and they did not recognize and accept Him. The prophets foretold Jesus' lineage and birth, ministry, suffering and death, and His resurrection and ascension.

Jesus told the Pharisees, "You search the Scriptures because you think that in them you have eternal life; and it is these that bear witness of Me; and you are unwilling to come to Me, that you may have life" (John 5:39). If they had been willing, He would have drawn them to Himself.

We too often embrace the Scriptures, the Word of God, and miss Jesus the living Word.

Could it be the American church is, in part, struggling in fleshly, often legalistic, self-effort because many of us have not recognized the time of our visitation by the Holy Spirit? Jesus in His last message before the cross, and before leaving this Earth, said His Spirit was not leaving us. This should give us great hope and life. The kingdom is where the King lives. How can His indwelling go unobserved?

~~~~~~~~~~~~~~~~~~~~~~~

He is as close as the mention of His name. As a new believer, someone gave me a book called Dominion over Demons. As I read, a spirit of fear came over me. I saw little dark forms moving around the room. I didn't know what or how to pray, so I cried out, "Jesus!" Immediately the demons disappeared, and eight angels stood around me. They were about seven feet tall and dressed in white. No words were spoken, but the unspoken word was "fear not," just as when angels appeared to people in the Bible. A total peace came over me, and I knew they were watching over my family also. I still like short prayers.

~~~~~~~~~~~~~~~~~~~~~~~~

Does prayer change things, or does *God* transform events? We often see undue emphasis on our faith and performance rather than God's faithfulness in us. For example, we hear: "You don't have enough faith, pray enough, or read your Bible enough." How much is enough? Do any of us ever measure up?

I hesitated to use negative statements to begin this book, yet I intend that this be a wake-up call to Christians. The majority of Americans claim to be Christians. However, many of these believe there are no absolute truths. It is common among professing Christians to live together outside of marriage. Examples of shallow faith abound.

> *The church in America is rightfully solid in its emphasis of righteousness imputed to us by faith in the finished work of Christ on the cross. I believe the church is weak in its emphasis of righteousness imparted to us by faith in the ongoing work of the indwelling Holy Spirit.*

God foretold His life being imparted to us by His indwelling Holy Spirit. "Moreover, I will give you a new heart and put a new spirit within you; and I will remove the heart of stone from your flesh and give you a heart of flesh. I will put My Spirit within you and *cause* you to walk in My statutes" (Ezekiel 36:26–27, emphasis mine). God did not intend that we would be forgiven, yet be struggling in sin. Jesus said, "It is to your advantage that I go away; for if I do not go away, the Helper will not come to you; but if I go, I will send Him to you" (John 16:7). Many are blind to the "glorious mystery, which is Christ in you, the hope of glory" (Colossians 1:27).

> *Have we gotten only half the good news?*

Author William Law in *The Power of the Spirit* states:

> The Holy Spirit's coming was no less to fulfill the Gospel than Christ's coming was the fulfillment of the Law and the Prophets. As all types and figures in the Law were but empty shadows without the coming of Christ, so the New Testament is but a dead letter without the Holy Spirit in redeemed men as the living power of a full salvation.

Jesus' last message before going to the cross (John 14–17) was, in part, an introduction to a New Covenant. Remember, Jesus came to Earth under the Old Covenant and taught and preached to those under the Old Covenant law. His words must be examined in that vein. However, here in Jesus' last message before the cross, He is speaking a message of grace to those who would be entering the age of grace. He was about to fulfill the law so we could live by grace.

Near the end of John 13, Peter assured Jesus he would die for Him. Jesus said, no, Peter would deny Him, saying, "Do not let your heart be troubled" (John 14:1). These are beautiful words of comfort, and what better words to introduce the New Covenant. Yes, here Jesus tries to prepare His disciples for a whole new way of life, not in His absence, but in His Spirit's presence. He was about to fulfill the Old Covenant, and the law, and usher in the New Covenant. He is the sacrifice required for our sin. His Spirit in us is the holiness required by the Law. He dealt with both the penalty and power of sin.

Why shouldn't Peter's heart be troubled when he was about to deny the Lord? Because though Peter would fail then, he would soon receive power after the Holy Spirit came upon him, and be Christ's witness, living by this indwelling Life. He would both live and die for Jesus in the power of the Spirit.

Jesus said He was going to prepare a dwelling place for us (John 14:3). As we study this message in context, we should see He was not speaking only, or even primarily, of a home in Heaven in the "sweet by and by."

> *Jesus has prepared a dwelling place in God for us, and in us for God.*

In *God Calling,* Jesus spoke to the authors, Two Listeners saying:

> Complete surrender of every moment to God is the foundation of happiness; the superstructure is the joy of communion with Him. And that is, for each, the place, the mansion, I went to

prepare for you. My followers have misunderstood that and looked too often upon that promise as referring only to the after-life.

In the *first few verses* of John 14, Jesus speaks of our dwelling place with Him in Heaven. In the *rest* of this long message, He speaks of dwelling with us here on Earth. John 15 emphasizes the fruit of the Spirit as we abide in Him. Jesus expressed His desire for oneness with us both at the beginning (John 14:3) and at the end (John 17:24) of this message.

> *He longs for a relationship with us here on Earth on our way to Heaven.*

Jesus promised them and us an indwelling God, answered prayer, keeping of Jesus' commandments, fruitfulness, and greater works than Jesus did—all these things, as well as persecution, and more. In these chapters Jesus states we will have another Helper who will be in us, and we in Him. Jesus will disclose Himself to us in this way. He will teach us and give us joy and peace.

So let us examine this place Jesus has prepared for us, the place of His abiding presence.

2. THE PLACE OF PREPARATION

In My Father's house are many dwelling places; if it were not so, I would have told you; for I go to prepare a place for you (John 14:2).

Where did Jesus go to prepare a place for us? Many would quickly say He went to Heaven. Are we to believe that Jesus took his carpenter tools and went to Heaven to prepare us a dwelling place? Was Heaven so imperfect that it needed preparation? The NIV translation of this verse can be misleading. It reads, "... I am going *there* to prepare a place for you" (John 14:2).

"There" is not in the original language. Was the preparation work Jesus did for us done in Heaven or on the cross? I think the Scriptures are clear. He went to the cross to buy our pardon with His precious blood. So the dwelling place prepared and the place of preparation are two different locations.

Jesus, our High Priest, did go to Heaven to offer His blood sacrifice to the Father, but His finished work of preparing a place for us was done at the cross. We have no place with God apart from the cross. Sin had separated us from the presence of God. Jesus, the Lamb of God, is both the blood sacrifice and the High Priest who offered it to God. "For Christ did not enter a holy place made with hands, a mere copy of the true one, but into Heaven itself, now to appear in the presence of God for us" (Hebrews 9:24). As a result of Christ's finished work on the cross our sins are forgiven, and we have a dwelling place prepared for us with God in Heaven, as well as the place of His abiding presence here on Earth.

THE WAY

In John 14:4–6 Jesus said, "And you know the way where I am going." Thomas said to Him, "Lord, we do not know where you are going, how do we know the way?" Jesus said to him, "I am the way, and the truth, and the life; no one comes to the Father but through Me."

Under the Old Covenant, only the high priest could enter into the Holy of Holies, into the presence of God, and then only with a blood sacrifice for the sins of the people and his own sins. Anyone coming any other way would be struck dead. Under the New Covenant, the blood of Jesus is the way into the Holy place where God dwells. When Jesus died on the cross, the veil in the Holy of Holies of the temple separating God from man was torn from top to bottom, from God to man. When we could not come to where God was, He came to us through the blood of His Son, Christ Jesus. "Therefore let us draw near with confidence to the throne of grace, so that we may receive mercy and find grace to help in time of need" (Hebrews 4:16).

~~~~~~~~~~~~~~~~~~~~~~~~~~~~~~

A great king once sat on his throne. No one could come into his presence unless invited or by permission. An exception was observed one day when his young son came storming into the room and jumped up on his daddy king's lap. We too can come boldly into our Papa God's presence since we are His children, joint heirs with Jesus (Romans 8:17).

~~~~~~~~~~~~~~~~~~~~~~~~~~~~~~

Notice we only draw near to God through Christ the way. He said, "...no one comes to the Father but through Me" (John 14:6). He is the way, the only way. By our faith in His finished work on the cross, Christ prepares a place in us for His Holy Spirit, imparting His righteousness to us, "... by the washing of regeneration and renewing of the Holy Spirit" (Titus 3:5).

THE TRUTH

What does it mean to be a believer? Going to church and believing the Bible is true won't save you. Head knowledge won't do. Salvation is found only in trusting in Jesus, the living Word. The written Word only points us to Him.

I used to think I must die first and go to Heaven to experience eternal life. Even though we will experience eternal life there, the phrase "eternal life in Heaven" is not in the Bible. In the Scriptures eternal life is always centered in the person of Jesus Christ (1 John 5:11–12, John 3:16, 36, Romans 6:23).

THE LIFE

The Scriptures also bear witness of the Holy Spirit, our indwelling life. Jesus tells His disciples in John 14:17 the Holy Spirit had been with them under the Old Covenant, but under the New Covenant He would be in them. So Christ in us by the Holy Spirit provides the righteous life required by the Law. "For if while we were enemies we were reconciled to God through the death of His Son, much more, having been reconciled, we shall be saved by His life" (Romans 5:10). J. B. Phillips New Testament renders this "… salvation through his living in us." Jesus' work on the cross is finished. His work on earth is not.

> *Yes, saved by His life, as well as by His death. The Holy Spirit is God's imparted life to us. Too often we only hear of being saved by His death.*

Jesus said, "You are to be perfect, as your Heavenly Father is perfect" (Matthew 5:48). He left us wondering how. That's a seeming impossibility, but in this discourse, Jesus prays to the Father, "I in them and You in Me, that they may be perfected in unity…" (John 17:23). He and the Father have made their home with us (John 14:23). We are not perfect in our performance. We are perfect or complete in Him, lacking nothing (Colossians2:9–10).

> *He is our indwelling perfection.*

An old hymn, Solid Rock states: "…dressed in His righteousness alone, faultless to stand before the throne." The only way we can stand in His presence is faultless, and faultless perfection is in Him alone, "…so that the requirement of the Law might be fulfilled in us, who do not walk according to the flesh but according to the Spirit" (Romans 8:4).

~~~~~~~~~~~~~~~~~~~~~~~~~~~

After clearly seeing the life of Christ in a Bible study leader, I hungered for this Savior and was fed the Bread of life. Seeing the need for Christian works and fruit in my life, I tried to produce it. One morning I overslept. No time to read my Bible and pray. Asking God's forgiveness, I grabbed one verse from a plastic bread loaf. It read, "It is vain for you to rise up early, to retire late, to eat the bread of painful labors; for He gives to His beloved even in his sleep" (Psalm 127:2). God does have a sense of humor. I needed a wake-up call. I got a grace awakening. I learned even when I'm not faithful to give Him my time, He is faithful to give me His time. Isn't faith just trust in His faithfulness?

~~~~~~~~~~~~~~~~~~~~~~~~~~~

Essentially, Jesus prepared a dwelling place with God for us, here and in Heaven, by fulfilling the Law. He said He did not come to abolish the Law but to fulfill it (Matthew 5:17). How did Jesus fulfill the Law? First, Jesus provided the blood sacrifice for sin required by the Law. Also, He serves as the mediator between God and man according to the Law. (Hebrews 8:6). Finally, Jesus is the righteousness required by the Law. He lives within us by the Holy Spirit to be our righteousness when we are born of God. In these ways Jesus fulfilled the law and thereby prepared a place for us with God, are all substantiated in this last message of His before the cross in John chapters fourteen through seventeen.

In John 13:36 Jesus told His disciples, "Where I go, you cannot follow Me now; but you will follow later." Was Jesus saying they would follow Him later to Heaven or to the cross, or both? They would follow Him to Heaven, yet, History indicates all His disciples except John were martyred for their faith in Him, some on crosses. As His followers, not all of us will have to be martyred, but Jesus did say, "If anyone wishes to come after Me, he must deny himself, and take up his cross daily and follow Me" (Luke 9:23). Taking up our cross means following Jesus come what may.

3. THE DWELLING PLACES

In My Father's house are many dwelling places; if it were not so, I would have told you; for I go to prepare a place for you. If I go and prepare a place for you, I will come again and receive you to Myself, that where I am, there you may be also (John 14:2–3).

In the previous chapter, we looked at the place of preparation, where Jesus went to prepare a place for us with God, namely the cross. In this chapter we will look at our dwelling places with God He prepared for us.

Traditionally, we have thought the place He has prepared for us was in Heaven. As Christians, we all look forward to going to Heaven after our physical death or at Christ's return to Earth. The Bible describes Heaven as a place of no more tears, trials, or troubles. When Christ receives us to Himself, we will see Him face to face and forever enjoy our time with Him. Clearly, this place in Heaven is what He is referring to in the first few verses of John 14.

24

However, the rest of this long message of Jesus refers primarily to our place in God's presence here on Earth.

He desires for us to live in the Heavenly realm on our way to Heaven. Author-teacher Malcolm Smith in *The Lost Secret of the New Covenant* states:

> The Holy Spirit inducts us into the world of the New Covenant called 'Heavenly places,' . . . for by the Spirit we are living moment by moment in Christ . . . God becomes the believer's habitat even as the believer becomes the dwelling of God . . . Even if, through ignorance, we have not yet lived in its power this is our address: in Christ.

We are His body, His many dwelling places on earth.

It is interesting to me Jesus never uses the word "Heaven" in these five chapters of John. He speaks of the Holy Spirit and His work and life in us throughout the message. Jesus did prepare a place for us in Heaven, and He went to the cross to do this. In this message, John 14–17, He is not speaking of Heaven only in the future physical sense "in the sweet by and by." I began to see it was not so much dwelling with Him now *as opposed to*—dwelling with Him in Heaven, but Heaven in us and we in Heaven in the here and now, as well as eternally.

> Scripture places our being in Heaven firmly in the *now* . . . the kingdom of Heaven is a spiritual realm all around us, which though it cannot be seen with human eyes is totally real. This is what Jesus meant when He told Nicodemus, who was expecting a literal government to appear on Earth, that the kingdom of God cannot be 'seen' by human eyes. It is invisible, like the wind. You enter it by becoming a spiritual person . . . How many believers fail to realize their inheritance in the kingdom *today* because they have been taught to live only for the return of Christ (D. Thomas Lancaster, *The Mystery of the Gospel*).

When Jesus prayed, "Father, I desire that they also, whom You have given Me, be with Me where I am" (John 17:24), He meant now and forever (Thy kingdom come...on Earth as it is in Heaven), not just after His second coming. He also said He would never leave us (Hebrews 13:5). No, we don't have to wait until we get to Heaven to be with Him. We are His body through whom His Spirit actively works on Earth.

While in Bible College I prayed for God's will in my life. *Lord, what ministry are you preparing me for? Where do You want me to serve you? What is your will for me?* Finally, the Lord spoke to my heart saying,

> *I am the will of God!*

I learned that God's will is not centered in a ministry or place. When we get our focus centered in Him, we will naturally, though supernaturally led, find ourselves in the right place, at the right time, doing the right thing.

When the Scriptures refer to "Heaven," they may be speaking of any of three places. 1. The sky. 2. Where the Father dwells. 3. The spiritual realm surrounding us. This last meaning is referred to in Ephesians 2:5–6. It states God has "…made us alive together with Christ (by grace you have been saved), and raised us up with Him, and seated us with Him in the Heavenly places in Christ Jesus," or literally in the Heavenlies. *Places* is not in the original language. It is not so much a place as it is a spiritual realm. Ephesians 6:12 also refers to, "…spiritual forces of wickedness in the Heavenly places." Since there are no spiritual forces of wickedness in Heaven, it must mean the Heavenlies or spiritual realm around us.

When John the Baptist said, "The kingdom of Heaven is at hand" (Matthew 3:2), he meant King Jesus was there. The kingdom is where the King dwells. That is why Jesus said, "The kingdom of Heaven is within you" (Luke 17:21). As believers, He reigns in our hearts. His Spirit is the atmosphere in which we find spiritual life.

"The death of Christ applied to the believer cuts him off from 'things Earthly,' so that he lives his life, henceforth, as one who abides in Heaven" (Jessie Penn-Lewis, *Dying to Live*). When we are living in Christ and He in us, we are seated with Him in the Heavenly spiritual realm. Andrew Murray in *God's Best Secrets* states:

> The first man who was brought forth from God had the breath of the Father, Son, and Holy Spirit breathed into him, and so he became a living soul . . . he was in the image and likeness of God because the Holy Trinity had breathed their own nature and Spirit into him. And as the Deity is always in Heaven . . . so this Spirit, breathed into man, brought Heaven into man along with it.

"Test yourselves to see if you are in the faith; examine yourselves. Or do you not recognize this about yourselves that Christ is in you— unless indeed you fail the test" (2 Corinthians 13:5).

> *Christ not in us is a*
> *Christ not ours.*

Of course, those of us in whom He lives need an ever greater revelation of this fact. It is too glorious to be fully comprehended by our finite minds. In many ways (John 17:21, Colossians1:27), Jesus tries to show us He was going to the cross to prepare a place for us here and now.

> *God prepared a place in*
> *Christ for us and a place*
> *in us for Christ.*

Unfortunately, many have little interest in this topic because they are satisfied with only a ticket to Heaven, or "fire insurance." God is *here*. I pray the Lord will reveal some of the beauty of "Christ in you, the hope of glory" (Colossians 1:27) in the *here and now*.

In 1 John 3:2 we read of future glorification. "We know that when He appears, we will be like Him." Jesus also spoke of present glorification. "The glory which you have given Me I have given to them [a done deal] that they may be one, just as We are one" (John 17:22). He in us is glorious.

Looking forward to Heaven is great, but if we have little or no connection or relationship with Him at this time, what makes us think we will in Heaven? Our problem is we often focus so much on our future in Heaven with Him, that we don't enjoy Him more on Earth.

4. **DWELLING IN CHRIST**

The glory which You have given to Me I have given to them, that they may be one just as We are one. I in them and You in Me, that they may be perfected in unity (John 17:22-23).

While dwelling with Jesus in Heaven is our ultimate goal, living in and with Him here on earth was the focus of Jesus' last message before the cross in John 14–17.

In John 14:2–3 Jesus states, "In My Father's house are many dwelling places; if it were not so, I would have told you; for I go to prepare a place for you. If I go and prepare a place for you, I will come again and receive you to Myself, that where I am, there you may be also." At Christ's first coming He went to the cross to die for us, to prepare a place in Heaven for us. At His second coming He will take us to that dwelling place. I think we get that. Do we see His other coming to us, the coming of His Spirit to make *us* His dwelling place? If so, what difference does it make in our lives?

The same Greek word for "dwelling place" is used only one more time in the New Testament, in John 14:23 where it is translated "abode". "If anyone loves Me, he will keep my word; and My Father will love him, and we will come to him and make Our abode with him." What a wonderful, glorious promise, the Father and Son living with and in us. He has prepared homes for Himself and us in this life and the next. Jesus, Eternal Life, lives in us.

Jesus' finished work on the cross prepared our way (He is the Way, John 14:6) into the Holy of Holies, into the very presence of God. "...no one comes to the Father but through Me" (14:7).

Jesus also promises us the Holy Spirit in John 14:16–17. "I will ask the Father, and He will give you another Helper..." The Spirit was with them in the person of Jesus but soon would reside in them. They went from being confused followers to becoming empowered apostles. Watchman Nee in *The Normal Christian Life* writes:

> Why is it that some of God's children live victorious lives while others are in a state of constant defeat? . . . some recognize His indwelling and others do not. True our victory lies in hiding in Christ, and in counting in simple trust upon His Holy Spirit . . . The Cross has been given to procure salvation for us;

the Spirit has been given to produce salvation in us.

We are new creations, not just forgiven. Too often we have been given only half a Gospel, focusing only on the cross. His indwelling is often all but ignored.

> *The cross makes us fit for Heaven. The Spirit makes us fit for earth.*

Jesus said, "I will not leave you as orphans; I will come to you" (John 14:18). Literally, this would read, "I am coming to you." How? He was coming to them in the continual presence of the Holy Spirit, not just for a short time before His ascension and not just at His second coming. An orphan is a fatherless child. God's children have an ever present Lord and Father. In His last words to them in Matthew 28:20, He states, "I am with you always, even to the end of the age." Do we believe Hebrews 13:5? "I will never desert you, nor will I ever forsake you."

The Lord's presence with us is not just a sentiment. We could say in a sense He is with us physically also, since the Bible says we are the body of Christ, in whom He dwells. He is the living Head of the body. Being in the presence of Christians is being in the presence of Christ. He is the sweetness in Christian fellowship.

Jesus goes on to say, "After a little while the world will see Me no more, but you will see Me; because I live, you will live also" (John 14:19). The world would see Him no more after His death, but after His resurrection, His disciples would see Him with their physical eyes. Those who experience His resurrection life in them have their spiritual eyes opened to see Him.

Jesus continues, "...because I live, you will live also. In that day you will know that I am in the Father and you in Me, and I in you" (John 14:20). In the day the Spirit infuses you with life, you will realize and experience this unity. As Christians, "our life in this world is actually His life lived in us" (1 John 4:17, *Phillips New Testament*).

We tend to sometimes try to put God in a box. We picture the Father in Heaven with Jesus sitting at His right hand. How can they be with us? Of course, the oneness and the Trinity of God cannot be fully comprehended by our finite minds. It might help to see God is Spirit, not *a* spirit. A spirit, like an angel, can only be in one place at a time. God is omnipresent, yet He is also present with believers in a special way. He is our domicile. He can be and do all we are incapable of doing on our own.

The Holy Spirit is sometimes referred to as the Spirit of Christ in the Bible. (Romans 8:9, 1 Peter 1:11). Also, Romans 8:11 tells us if the Spirit of the

Father dwells in us He will give life to our mortal bodies. Therefore the Trinity, Father, Son, and Spirit, is our habitation.

In John 14:21, Jesus states, "He who has My commandments and keeps them is the one who loves Me; and he who loves Me will be loved by My Father, and I will love him and disclose Myself [literally shine forth] to him." How? In many ways. He abides in us to have sweet fellowship with us, revealing Himself to us. Lest you think that Jesus was speaking of disclosing Himself at His second coming, notice He was not going to disclose Himself to the world (14:22). At His second coming "every eye will see Him" (Revelation1:7). Are you beginning to see an ever- present Trinity?

~~~~~~~~~~~~~~~~~~~~~~~~~~~~~

A few years ago, just before my wife, Rita, was wheeled into the operating room for surgery, I received an unusual phone call. A man we had met a few years earlier said God had told him to call and pray for Rita. He did not know that she was having surgery. After Rita's successful surgery, I asked a friend, "How did he know to call right before Rita's surgery? He didn't know she was having surgery. How did he get our phone number?" At that very moment, a man on television said, "But there is a God in

Heaven who reveals secrets" (Daniel 2:28, NKJV). Jesus does disclose Himself.

~~~~~~~~~~~~~~~~~~~~~~~~~~~~

"You have heard that I said to you, 'I go away, and I will come to you.' If you loved me you would have rejoiced because I go to the Father, for the Father is greater than I" (John 14:28). I believe the meaning of this is closely related to what Jesus said in John 16:7. "But I tell you the truth, it is to your advantage that I go away; for if I do not go away, the Helper will not come to you; but if I go, I will send Him to you." The Spirit was not the consolation prize since Jesus was leaving, but the very purpose of Jesus' coming, to give us life. Jesus came, died, rose, ascended, and sent His Spirit.

Andrew Murray in *God's Best Secrets* stated: "To Paul, the very center and substance of his Gospel was the indwelling Christ..." Dr. Alexander MacLaren, a Baptist preacher, once said that it seemed as if the church had lost the truth of the indwelling Christ." Is this truth still lost to most of the church of our day as well?

We are incomplete until Christ is living and working within us and through us. "For in Him the whole fullness of Deity (the Godhead) continues to dwell in bodily form [giving complete expression of the divine nature]. And you are in Him, made full and having come to fullness of life [in Christ you too are filled with the Godhead-Father, Son and Holy

Spirit—and reach full spiritual stature]..."
(Colossians2:9–10, ₐₘₚ). He completes us.

> *Two-thousand*
> *years ago, God*
> *walked the earth in*
> *Jesus of Nazareth*
> *and now He walks*
> *the earth in us, the*
> *body of Christ.*

In John fourteen, we see many testimonies to God's indwelling of us. Also in John chapter fifteen, Jesus speaks of us abiding in Him in order to bear the fruit of His Spirit (John 15:4–5). Apart from Him, whatever we do for Him, He says is nothing. Yet, abiding in Him we can do anything He asks of us, even greater works than He did (John 14:12). We will look at these subjects of greater works and fruitfulness later. For now, just notice Jesus uses the word "abide or abiding" nine times in the first ten verses of John fifteen. He must live in us and we in Him.

Major W. Ian Thomas in *The Indwelling Life Of Christ* states: "The Lord Jesus came from Heaven to Earth not just to get us out of hell and into Heaven...but to get Himself out of Heaven and into us. He gave Himself for us to give Himself to us."

In John 16:13, Jesus said, "But when He, the Spirit of truth, comes, He will guide you into all the truth." Remember, Jesus said He is the truth, so the Holy Spirit will guide us to Jesus, and abiding in Him, He will keep us from all error.

Moving on to John seventeen, we see Jesus emphasizing our unity with Him and the Father and each other. "...that they may all be one; even as you, Father, are in Me and I in You, that they also may be in Us, so that the world may believe that You sent Me... I in them and You in Me, that they may be perfected in unity..." (John 17:21, 23). He both imputes and imparts perfection to us.

Jesus goes on to pray in John 17:24, "Father, I desire that they also, whom You have given Me, be with Me where I am..." Since He is here, the prayer is for His presence with and in us here and eternally. Concluding in verse 26, Jesus prays, "...and I have made Your name known to them, and will make it known, so that the love wherewith You loved Me may be in them and I in them." He makes the Father's name, indicating His nature, known to us by making His nature to dwell within us. "I in them" sums it up. What a Savior!

5. EVIDENCE FOR THE INDWELLING

I have been crucified with Christ; and it is no longer I who live, but Christ lives in me; and the life which I now live in the flesh I live by faith in the Son of God, who loved me and gave Himself up for me (Galatians 2:20).

Jesus introduced the New Covenant with the promise of the coming Holy Spirit. His apostles carried on this teaching in the power of His life. Apparently, the indwelling life of Christ cannot be emphasized enough in the New Testament. Not only does Jesus stress this truth in His last message before the cross, but all the New Testament writers also confirm this indispensable good news.

So why is it so little preached and taught? Is it because of shallow faith or unbelief? No condemnation there. We all need more faith. If asked, most Christians would say they know Jesus lives within them. Yet, often there is so little evidence of this fact in our lives. Why? We haven't relinquished control to Him. We haven't died to self.

So instead of manifesting Himself in our lives, He hides Himself. He will not share His glory with another(Isaiah 42:8). Yet, He intends the glory of His presence be seen in us.

~~~~~~~~~~~~~~~~~~~~~~~~~~~~~~

Rita and I volunteered several times at Calvary Commission, a home and school for Christian ex-convicts in Lindale, Texas. While speaking at their chapel service, the Lord laid it on my heart that *He does not live in condemned houses.* These former drug addicts and alcoholics used to be like abandoned, empty, condemned houses. Now God has built them into holy dwellings of the Most High God. He has filled them with His presence, and they cannot contain Him. He spills out through their eyes, smiles, and testimonies. We are not slum lords.

~~~~~~~~~~~~~~~~~~~~~~~~~~~~~~

Jesus also could not make people believe He was indwelt by the Father. Jesus said, "Do you not believe that I am in the Father, and the Father is in Me? The words that I say to you I do not speak on My own initiative, but the Father abiding in Me does His works. Believe Me that I am in the Father and the Father is in Me" (John 14:10).

> *In the 21 chapters of John's Gospel, more than 42 times Jesus said or inferred that He did and said nothing except what the Father told Him.*

When Jesus stresses something this many times, it must be important. He lived by the life of the Father. We are to live by the life of the Spirit of our Father as well. Christianity is supernatural. We were recreated, filled with the Spirit, anointed to speak His thoughts and do His works.

Martyr Margaret Wilson was pressured to recant her faith in Christ. She said, 'I cannot speak the word that dishonors Jesus.' They tied her to a stake and floated her in the sea. They tied another grey haired old saint to another stake and put her in the sea. They said, 'Won't you now recant? Don't you see her agony? She said, 'No, I do not see her; I only see Jesus in His suffering servant wrestling there (Dr. A. B. Simpson, founder of The Christian and Missionary Alliance, *The Christ Life*).

The Father was in Jesus, and yet Jesus was going to the Father. It is a bit of a paradox. The Lord lives in us, and yet we will one day go to be with Him? Yet, this is the heart of the gospel, an ever-present indwelling God. Let us look at some of the Scripture analogies that describe our life in union with Christ.

THE BODY OF CHRIST

Paul's amazing prayer for the church expresses the reality of God in us. He prayed we would be a body "completely filled and flooded with God Himself" (Ephesians 3:19, Amp).

We have "the fullness of Him who fills all in all" (Ephesians 1:23). While there are many members of the body of Christ with various gifts and functions, apart from Him, we can do nothing. Could it look like Him in action when we are not apart from Him?

It is His body to do with as He pleases. We are not our own. From the head or brain come the impulses that direct the members of the body to function in an orderly fashion. "Take my hands and let them move, at the impulse of Thy love" (Frances R. Havergal). Our hands are like God's gloves, nothing in themselves until filled with His love, life, and direction.

God expresses Himself in unique ways through each of us. We all have a ministry to perform in unity with Him. This is possible only through "this mystery among the Gentiles, which is Christ in you, the hope of glory. We proclaim Him, admonishing every man and teaching every man with all wisdom, so that we may present every man complete in Christ (Colossians 1:27-28).

The body of Christ is not just like a body, but is a true body, a spiritual organism. "For just as we have many members in one body and all the members do not have the same function, so we, who are many, are one body in Christ, and individually members one of another" (Romans 12:4–5).

> *The purpose of the body is that the Son of God would continue to have an incarnation to express His life.*

The incarnation was the uniting of God with humanity through Christ. This is why Jesus told His disciples it was better for Him to go away that the Holy Spirit would come to live within them, making them the body of Christ. Now His body is able to work around the globe, rather than just in Israel.

TREASURE IN EARTHEN VESSELS

There is a price to be paid for this indwelling life of Christ. "For we who live are constantly being delivered over to death for Jesus' sake, so that the life of Jesus also may be manifested in our mortal flesh" (2 Corinthians 4:11). "But we have this treasure in Earthen vessels, so that the surpassing greatness of the power will be of God and not from ourselves" (2 Corinthians 4:7). Jesus is the treasure in these Earthen vessels, our bodies. Oh, that He would shine forth more.

God formed man out of the dust of the ground and breathed His life into us. When man fell into sin, we lost that indwelling life or breath of God. Christ came to Earth to die so we might once again be filled with the Spirit of God. Right before the cross, Jesus promised the Holy Spirit. Right after He rose from the dead, Jesus breathed on His disciples and said to them, "Receive the Holy Spirit" (John 20:22). Under the new covenant, man is restored to life with God by the breath or Spirit of God.

> *We are vessels of honor holding precious Treasure.*

THE HOUSE OF GOD

"Christ was faithful as a Son over His house—whose house we are" (Hebrews 3:6). "the Most High does not dwell in temples made by human hands" (Acts 17:28). The true church is not a building or an organization controlled by the rules of men but a holy collection of living stones with Jesus Christ as the cornerstone. "In Him we live, and move, and have our being" (Acts 17:28). That's better than living in an RV.

A. B. Simpson in *The Christ Life* writes: "It is not fixing up the house that we need. Give Christ the vacant lot, and He will excavate below the old life and build a worthier house, where He will live forever . . . he will bring His own holiness and come and dwell in our hearts forever." We are part of God's family, and our Father lives as Head of the family. "So then you are… of God's household… a dwelling of God in the Spirit" (Ephesians 2:19). If we are His house, maybe we need to practice hospitality, enjoying His presence and inviting others.

It is important to see that God's household is not me, but we. We find Him in each other. Each member manifests different gifts or characteristics of the Lord. We need each other. There are no "Lone Rangers" in Christ's household or body.

THE TEMPLE OF THE HOLY SPIRIT

"Do you not know that you are a temple of God and that the Spirit of God dwells in you?" (1 Corinthians3:16) The Old Testament temple was just a type of the one in Heaven. What made the temple holy was the presence of the Holy God. The finished work of Christ on the cross and His presence in us is what makes us holy. It is not our performance. We are not improved but filled, making us new creations (2 Corinthians 5:17). "For we are the temple of the living God; just as God said, 'I will dwell in them and walk among them'" (2 Corinthians 6:16). While Christ was on Earth, He was the temple filled with the Spirit of God. That is why He said, "Destroy this temple, and in three days I will raise it up" (John 2:19). Now we are the temple that God inhabits with His Spirit and our spirit in harmony.

> *We are not improved, but new creations. His glory fills these temples.*

Jesus prayed to the Father, "The glory which You have given Me I have given to them) John 17:22.In 2 Corinthians 6:19 it states this temple belongs to God. We are such meager temples for the glorious Shekinah presence of God.

In a blood covenant, the animal blood sacrifice was split into two parts, and both parties to the covenant walked between the two halves. When Jesus was sacrificed for our sin the veil in the temple representing our sin which separated us from the presence of God was split in two, from top to bottom, from God to man. Under the New Covenant, we walk through the blood of Jesus into God's presence. By one offering we come near to God. By offering Him as the Way, the Truth and the Life, we come near to others.

BREAD OF HEAVEN

"Jesus then said to them, 'Truly, truly, I say to you, it is not Moses who has given you the bread out of Heaven, but it is My Father who gives you the true bread out of Heaven" (John 6:32). "I am the bread of life; he who comes to Me will not hunger, and he who believes in Me will never thirst" (Vs.35). "He who eats My flesh and drinks My blood abides in Me and I in him" (Vs.56).

There is that word "abides" again. Abide means to stay. Jesus is speaking of the spiritual food of His life in us. When we are born again, and the Holy Spirit comes to live within us, we have "become partakers of the divine nature…" (2 Peter 1:4). We are well fed. Are we sharing this life-giving nourishment with spiritually starving people?

> *The supernatural is our
> second nature.*

OTHER EVIDENCE

With so much scriptural evidence for an indwelling Lord, the question keeps arising in my mind, why is this truth so little taught in our churches and Christian colleges? Why so little evidence of God's presence in the lives of His children? I suspect we are trying to live as Christians naturally or in the power of the flesh. The gifts of the Spirit are just that, *of the Spirit.* Is this why we seldom see people healed or raised from the dead? Is anything too difficult for a supernatural indwelling God? Jesus said, "you are to stay [abide] in the city until you are clothed with power from on high" (Luke 24:49).

Many Christian writers of today are quite shallow, I believe. I call some of them "book factories." Some are prolific writers but may lack depth. Writers of Christian classics of days gone by certainly focused on God's indwelling: Andrew Murray, A. W. Tozer, A. B. Simpson, Watchman Nee, F. B. Meyer, D. L. Moody, Frances Havergal, Hannah Whithall Smith, Hudson Taylor and Madame Guyon, to name just a few, led transformed lives only after experiencing God's presence, and wrote of this. William Law's earlier writing (legalism), compared with his later writing, show he had a revelation of Christ later in life.

The writings and lives of classic Christian writers of the past have sharpened my hunger for a deeper walk with the Lord. Their lives have convicted me of my own lack of depth in comparison to theirs. "But when they measure themselves by themselves and compare themselves with themselves, they are without understanding" (2 Corinthians 10:12).

However, if we measure self against the indwelling life of Christ, we find no good thing in self (Romans 7:18). He lives in us not to improve self, but so we would despair of self, and desire Him to be our life. "until we all attain to the unity of the faith, and of the knowledge of the Son of God, to a mature man, to the measure of the stature which belongs to the fullness of Christ" (Ephesians 4:13).

Probably the greatest evidence for the indwelling Savior is the transformation from being self-centered to Christ-centered lives. A poem by A. B. Simpson from *The Christ Life* conveys this Christ-centered life he found:

> Once it was the blessing, now it is the Lord; Once it was the feeling, now it is His Word; Once His gifts I wanted, now the Giver own; Once I sought healing, now Himself alone. Once 'twas painful trying, now 'tis perfect rest;

Once a half salvation, now the uttermost . . . Once the power I wanted, now the Mighty One; Once for self I labored, now for Him alone.

6. THE WAY

I am the way, and the truth, and the life; no one comes to the Father, but through Me (John 14:6).

Certainly, there is a way for all of us to know God intimately, not just a select few. While few find this way, He's readily available to all, for the way is not a method or a technique. Jesus Himself is this way. After Jesus had said, "And you know the way where I am going" (John 14:4), Thomas said, "Lord, we do not know where you are going, how do we know the way?" (John 14:4–5) While the disciples didn't understand the big picture yet, they did know Jesus, even if inadequately.

~~~~~~~~~~~~~~~~~~~~~~~~~~~~

I found Jesus to be the way only after going the wrong way for many years. While needing a relationship with Jesus, I grew up with only religion. Trusting in my performance did not keep me from sin. Trusting in Jesus' performance on the cross and the Holy Spirit's performance within me I found the way, a walk of grace in the power of the Spirit. Grace is His unmerited favor in action in our lives. In Bible college, some professors merely taught truth. In others, I saw the Way, the Truth, and the Life, Jesus.

~~~~~~~~~~~~~~~~~~~~~~~~~~~~

Jesus did not give methods, biblical principles, rules, or laws as "the way." He gave Himself on the cross, and He was soon to give us Himself in the person of the Holy Spirit who guides us in all our ways.

~~~~~~~~~~~~~~~~~~~~~~~~~~~~

"The road's flooded!"

My wife and I were on our way to a Bible study when we came upon a flooded road in rural Indiana. She exclaimed, "We are not driving through high water." We back-tracked to the little village of Gosport. I pulled to the side of the road to look at my map. As I did so, a young lady walked out of the woods and over to our car.

"Can I help you?" she asked.

I told her I was checking my map to

see if we could get to our destination on the road ahead. She said we could not go that way due to a washed-out bridge. She gave us an alternate way to our destination. We were greatly relieved that we had not driven off that bridge.

We arrived at the Bible study and shared what had happened. Friends there asked what this young lady looked like. We described her to those who lived in the tiny town of Gosport. They said there was no one in that little community who looked like that. Was she an angel, sent to deliver us from danger or death? Some day we may find out. Whether human or angelic, we believe she was sent by Jesus, the Way, to warn us of going the wrong way.

~~~~~~~~~~~~~~~~~~~~~~~~~~~~

Prayer and Bible study are not the way to Jesus, but Jesus is the way to give life to prayer and Bible study.

If we look to our doing as the way, we will be continually frustrated. Doing should follow being,

being in Christ that is.

Satan always has a very attractive plan B. Religious activity is perhaps his most popular device. It didn't work for the Pharisees, and it won't work for us. "There is a way that seems right to man, but its end leads to death" (Proverbs 14:12). We need to stay on the narrow one-way street.

Popular contemporary author John Eldridge, in *Waking The Dead*, questions why many large churches have so many programs:

> Their plan for discipleship involves, first becoming a member . . . attending Sunday morning service and a small group fellowship. Complete a course on evangelism . . . doctrine . . . finances . . . marriage . . . parenting . . . leadership . . . hermeneutics . . . spiritual gifts . . . Biblical counseling. Participate in missions. Carry a significant local church ministry 'load.' You're probably surprised I would question this sort of program . . . a great deal of helpful information is passed on. My goodness, you could earn an MBA with less effort . . . they master Christian precepts and miss the most important thing . . . intimacy with God.

I think anyone involved in church programs this intensely has little time for God Himself.

I wonder how many churches tell their people sitting at Jesus' feet like Mary is more important than serving Him like Martha. Coming to Jesus is more important than coming to church, even though church attendance is important. Paul's teaching on the principle of giving emphasized helping people more than just programs. Eldridge also states:

> Then there are the systems aimed at getting your behavior in line . . . an unspoken list of what you shouldn't do . . . (typically rather long) and a list of what you may (usually much shorter) . . . and leaves us only exhausted. And this we are told is the good news . . . When it doesn't strike us as something to get excited about, we feel we must not be spiritual enough . . . We don't need more facts . . . more things to do. We need Life, and we've been looking for it ever since we lost Paradise.

We have been eating from the wrong tree ever since Eden. We keep trying to find life from the tree of the Knowledge of Good and Evil, rather than Jesus, the Tree of Life. Jesus bids us, come, take and eat. Trying to live by the Ten Commandments rather than the indwelling life of Christ is like eating from the tree of the Knowledge of Good and Evil. The

Law shows us what good and evil are but does not equip us to obey. Only the Holy Spirit can do so.

Many legalists might be surprised to hear the "law is not made for a righteous person, but for those who are lawless and rebellious, for the ungodly and sinners" (1 Timothy 1:9). Second Corinthians 3:6 tells us the letter of the law kills, but the Spirit gives life.

The Law showed us our inability to come to God. When we couldn't come to Him, He came to us in the person of Jesus, and He is still here. If we see our need of Him and desire Him to meet that need, He will do the rest. "Commit your way to the Lord, trust also in Him, and He will do it" (Psalm 37:5).

> *Trying to live by the Ten Commandments rather than the indwelling life of Christ is like eating from the tree of the Knowledge of Good and Evil.*

Whenever eternal life is mentioned in Scripture, it is always centered in Jesus. Many people know their Bible without knowing their Lord very well. We come to God looking for answers. He shows us Himself.

Not only is Jesus the way to the Father, but He also is the destination. Jesus is the Way into the presence of God, and He Himself is that Presence. Jesus is not only the way to blessings but the greatest blessing of all. "But by His doing you are in Christ Jesus, who *became* to us, wisdom from God, and righteousness and sanctification, and redemption" (1 Corinthians 1:30, emphasis mine). He is our all in all.

Previously, Rita and I lived in college towns. In these schools of so-called "higher learning," the notion prevailed there are many ways to God. We are told by the world to believe in only one way is to be intolerant. What then are we to do with Jesus' statement that He is the *only* way? If He was wrong, He would not be God. Either He is the only way, or He is no way.

Jesus said, "However, when the Son of Man comes, will He find faith on the Earth" (Luke 18:8)? The fact Jesus is the only way makes it a narrow way. Jesus said, "For the gate is small and the way is narrow that leads to life, and there are few who find it" (Matthew 7:14). So when people say Christians are narrow-minded, we can say, "That's right." To be politically correct, we are told not to pray in the name of Jesus, but we don't believe in a generic God.

A recent poll indicated two-thirds of evangelicals in the U. S. believe there is more than one way to God. "And there is salvation in no one else; for there is no other name under Heaven that has been given among men by which we must be saved" (Acts 4:12). Christianity is an exclusive way. While we should love people of all faiths, we must reject any false way to God—any way but Jesus. The best way to love all people is to share Christ with them.

Those of us His light has enlightened know Him to be the way. No amount of mental gymnastics could ever convince us otherwise. He does not give us life apart from Himself, but He Himself is our life (Colossians 3:4). If we really believe Him to be our life and the only way to God, shouldn't He be heard from and seen in us?

Another analogy Jesus used to show He is the Way was referring to Himself as the "Door." "I am the door; if anyone enters through Me, he will be saved, and will go in and out and find pasture" (John 10:9).

The early Christians were first called followers of *the Way*. Paul, speaking of his life before becoming a Christian said, "And I persecuted this Way to the death, binding and putting both men and women into prison" (Acts 22:4). When Paul found the Way, he too was persecuted. Persecution only serves to spread the gospel, as seen in China. The Communists tried to stamp out Christianity, kicking all missionaries out of the country after World War 2. The underground church multiplied all the more not only in spite of, but to a great extent because of persecution.

Mystic Madame Guyon in *Experiencing The Depths Of Jesus Christ* stated: "Abandonment is the

key to the inward spiritual life . . . it is to the Lord
Jesus that you abandon yourself . . . If you follow
Him as the Way, you will hear Him as the Truth, and
He will bring life to you as the Life."

Andrew Murray in *God's Best Secrets* shed light
on this Scripture:

> In the temple, there was a veil between
> the holy place and the Holiest of all . . .
> behind the veil, the high priest alone
> might enter once a year. This veil was
> the symbol of sinful human nature . . .
> when Christ died the veil was torn in
> two. Christ dedicated *'a new and living
> way'* to God through the torn veil of
> His flesh . . . The torn veil of the flesh
> refers not only to Christ and His
> sufferings, but also to our experience in
> the likeness of His sufferings. Is this
> not the reason why many Christians
> can never attain close fellowship with
> God? They have never yielded the flesh
> as an accursed thing to the
> condemnation of the cross . . . Christ
> has called us to hate our lives, to lose
> our lives, and to be dead with Him to
> sin so that we may live to God with
> Him . . . with the flesh crucified in
> Christ Jesus.

"We have confidence to enter the holy place by the blood of Jesus, by a new and living way which He inaugurated for us through the veil, that is, His flesh" (Hebrews 10:19–20). Jesus is the Way.

7. THE TRUTH

I am the way, and the truth, and the life; no one comes to the Father but through Me (John 14:6).

There are many seekers after truth. Some seek for truth in eastern religions, some through higher learning, and some in higher consciousness. Some look within themselves, and some look to false messiahs. Jesus is who they hunger for. So few know it and find Him.

The Pharisees thought they were authorities on the truth, yet, they could not recognize the Truth when He stood before them. Jesus called them blind leaders of the blind. Due to their pride, Jesus declared them guilty (Matthew 15:14, John 9:39–41).

He only comes to the needy heart.

The cross of Christ reveals to us the truth about sin, man, and God. The world doesn't see sin as such a big deal. The cross shows us how serious it is since the Lord of Glory had to die there for our sin. The only way to Jesus is through the cross, seeing our utter depravity. Both for salvation and for sanctification, we must see the truth, ourselves as abhorrent, and Jesus as our only righteousness.

The world sees man as basically good. The Apostle Paul says the opposite. "For I know that nothing good dwells in me" (Romans 7:18).

~~~~~~~~~~~~~~~~~~~~~~~~~~~~~~~

Growing up I believed the Scriptures to be totally true and Jesus was who the Bible said He was. This was not saving faith since the demons also believe this and shudder (James 2:19). I took sin lightly, believing God would forgive. As I lived a life of license to sin through a false idea of God's grace, a life of liberty in Christ awaited me. Even as I lived a lie, Jesus revealed Himself to me as the truth through a Bible study leader who glowed with His life and truth. I saw Christ in him and invited Him into me. I was born again. Later out of gratefulness to God, I then tried to live this supernatural life in the power of the flesh, until I had a grace awakening. I found rest for my soul in

Jesus. Our performance always comes up short. Life's not in trying but trusting.

~~~~~~~~~~~~~~~~~~~~~~~~~~~

Before and after being born again, we need a Savior to do for us what we cannot do for ourselves. He must bring us to the end of ourselves. Only then can we find our all-in-all in Him. We have a death grip on this life we think we possess. We don't die to self easily. He uses many loving, but often painful means to bring us to this point of surrender. Death must come before life. But then, "you will know the truth, and the truth will make you free" (John 8:32).

It's not in trying but trusting.

It's not in running but resting.

~~~~~~~~~~~~~~~~~~~~~~~~~~~

Rita and I volunteered twice at Calvary Commission in Lindale, Texas, a halfway house for released prisoners. These men and women have been born again while in prison. They know what it is to be free even while still in prison. When they sing, "Where the Spirit of the Lord is, there is freedom," they really belt out the words, "THERE IS FREEDOM." What a testimony to the power of God to free us from our past lives of sin and the things that bind us in the prisons of self.

~~~~~~~~~~~~~~~~~~~~~~~~~

> *Apart from Christ we can do nothing. United with Him all things are possible.*

Galatians 2:20 states, "I have been crucified with Christ; and it is no longer I who live, but Christ lives in me; and the life which I now live in the flesh I live by faith in the Son of God, who loved me and gave Himself up for me." We died with Him. His life ascends in us. We are not improved but replaced. We must see we died with Him, He lives in us, and He will live out His life through us. This has been called the exchanged life, by many writers of the deeper life.

> *Jesus died instead of us. He must live within instead of us.*

This is the "Law of the Spirit of Life in Christ Jesus" (Romans 8:2) that sets us free from the law of sin and death. The Spirit enlivens our mortality (Romans 8:11).

Sanctification is the work of the Holy Spirit. Not seeing God's active presence in us has led to all kinds of programs of reform, refinement, and legalism. Instead of seeing the fruit of the Spirit and the life of Christ manifested in our mortal bodies (2 Corinthians 4:11), we see people struggling to pray more, study harder, and have more faith. We always come up short in our own strength. "'Not by might nor by power, but by My Spirit' says the Lord of hosts" (Zechariah 4:6).

Another truth Jesus reveals is our nothingness apart from Him. He said, "apart from Me you can do nothing" (John 15:5). To see who we are in Christ, we must first see who we are apart from Him. Godly mystic Madame Guyon in *Experiencing the Depths of Jesus Christ* expressed it well:

> Dear reader, there are, in fact, only two truths: the All and the nothing. Everything else is a lie. God is All; You are nothing. The only way you can pay due honor to God is by your own annihilation. As soon as this wonderful work is done, God moves in . . . He comes to the place of nothingness, of emptiness, and instantly fills it with Himself. He puts Himself in the very

place of that which He has put to death.

The word truth is used *forty-four* times in John's Gospel and his three epistles. The truth is not just a body of information or doctrine. "And the Word was made flesh, and dwelt among us . . . full of grace and truth" (John 1:14, KJV). In 2nd and 3rd John knowing the truth and walking in the truth refers to Jesus. To be in Christ, to abide in Christ, is to walk in the truth by the Spirit of truth.

Knowing the truth, or knowing Jesus as the Truth, does not mean we might somehow figure God out and understand all His ways. God's ways are beyond our understanding. He states, in Psalm 50:21, "You thought that I was just like you." We better think again. The Lord set Job straight in this regard. God said, "Where were you when I laid the foundation of the Earth? Tell me, if you have understanding, who set its measurements? . . . Have you ever in your life commanded the morning?" (Job 38:4–5, 12). Even though we have the indwelling Spirit of God, He doesn't reveal everything to us. He keeps us dependent.

Standing before Pontus Pilate, Jesus told him, "For this I have been born, and for this I have come into the world, to testify to the truth. Everyone who is of the truth hears My voice." Pilate said to Him, "What is truth?" (John 18:37–38)

Biblical scholars and no one denomination have the corner on truth. With more than 41,000

Christian denominations, according to Global Christianity, how can we know what to believe? The Bible gives us some light on this. Jesus said we should come to Him in simple childlike trust. He will give us revelation.

It is possible to have a great deal of head knowledge of the Bible, without knowing Jesus as the Truth. "But a natural man does not accept the things of the Spirit of God, for they are foolishness to him; and he cannot understand them, because they are spiritually appraised [understood] . . . For who has known the mind of the Lord, that he will instruct Him? But we have the mind of Christ" (1 Corinthians 2:14–16). We have *His* mind, not a mind *like* Christ's or an imitation. His thoughts and desires can become ours. Correct doctrine won't keep us in Jesus. Jesus will keep us in correct doctrine. The Spirit sometimes uses human teachers to lead us to truth, but the Spirit is the one who brings things to life for us.

> *Correct doctrine won't keep us in Jesus.*
>
> *Jesus will keep us in correct doctrine.*

Gene Edwards in *Epilogue to Experiencing the Depths of Jesus Christ* states:

> The Old Testament told all about Christ, but when men read the Old Testament they did not see Him there. God is like that. He keeps His highest revelation slightly veiled. Why? So men will not trample it underfoot. But then one day Christ came. All at once God lifted the veil. Men could turn to the Old Testament and so easily see Christ all through it. But at the same time that God lifted the veil on the old, He did something else. He placed a veil over the new— Christ. While Christ lived on the Earth, God veiled all that His Son said. Men who heard Him could not quite get the full meaning of His words. Christ was veiled to all except His handful of disciples (and even His disciples did not fully understand until after their Lord came into them as Spirit to interpret all He had formally said) . . . He keeps His most precious things slightly veiled. He does this to keep the things dear to Him from being cheapened.

This is so true. Just as Jesus told Pilate, "Everyone who is of the truth hears My voice." We can only hear and discern spiritual truth when the Spirit of Truth lifts the veil so we can see. "whenever a person turns to the Lord, the veil is taken away. Now the Lord is the Spirit, and where the Spirit of the Lord is, there is liberty" (2 Corinthians 3:16–17). There is freedom to see. It is not to the spiritually elite that Christ is revealed, but to those with child-like faith.

Much of what Jesus said could not be understood until after His resurrection, and then only by those who believed in Him and had received the Holy Spirit. Many things He said could be taken more than one way. For example; "Destroy this temple and in three days I will rebuild it" (John 2:19). "You are clean, but not all of you" (John 13:10).

He said, "I will come again and receive you to Myself, that where I am, there you may be also" (John 14:10). Was He referring only to His second coming, or could He have also meant the coming of His Holy Spirit? We live this side of the cross and have the written word of the New Testament, the disciples did not have. We should understand much more than they. But do we? When I share the truth of the indwelling Christ as our life, people have said, "I've never heard that taught."

It comes down to need and desire. The Holy Spirit must first show us our emptiness without Christ, and then create the hunger for Christ within us. Like the Apostle Paul, we must have a Romans seven experience where we find we are incapable of doing the good we want. In our flesh dwells no good thing.

Jesus said, "Blessed are those who hunger and thirst for righteousness, for they shall be satisfied" (Matthew 5:6). "It is not those who are healthy who need a physician, but those who are sick" (Matthew 9:12). He reveals Himself to those who know they need help. Jesus in His last message before the cross shows us the way to truth; "But the Helper, the Holy Spirit, whom the Father will send in My name, He will teach you all things" (John 14:26). "He who loves Me will be loved by My Father, and I will love him and will disclose Myself to him" (John 14:21). "I have many more things to say to you, but you cannot bear them now. But when He, the Spirit of truth, comes, He will guide you into all the truth" (John 16:13). Christ is the truth. When we get centered on Him, He will reveal His hidden truth by manifesting Himself to us. That's the truth.

8. THE LIFE

*I am the way, and the truth, and the life; no
one comes to the Father but through Me (John
14:6).*

Jesus said, "I came that they may have life, and
have it abundantly" (John 10:10). This is the theme
of John's gospel. "...but these have been written so
that you may believe that Jesus is the Christ, the Son
of God; and that believing you may have life in His
name" (John 20:31). His "name" indicates His
power, authority, and nature. He has given us a new
nature, His nature. Abundant, eternal life is Christ in
us.

*The abundant life He is
was meant to be seen
in you, creating a hunger
in others for Him.*

John Eldredge in *Waking the Dead* writes: "It's life that He promised, and it's life that we need. The Resurrection gives us that life. How awesome it is to begin to discover through the power of the life of Christ in us, we are saved by His life" (Romans 5:10).

We usually focus on being saved by His death, but His indwelling Life saves us from a self-centered life, which is really death. As A. B. Simpson in *The Christ Life* put it: "Trust Christ, and live by Him until at last it comes as natural as breathing." He then becomes second nature to us.

~~~~~~~~~~~~~~~~~~~~~~~~~~~~~~~~~~

I Saw Life – My Testimony

Christ came to be my indwelling life after taking me through painful dying experiences. Before eternal life could enliven me, I had to be taken to death. While I served with the Army in Vietnam, news came that my best friend was wounded and not expected to live. Devastated, I cried out to God. He lived but is partially paralyzed.

While sick with Crohn's disease and unhappy, I thought I was a Christian. Down to 100 pounds, I was evacuated and underwent surgery. My health returned for a season. Seven years later another surgery for Crohn's was needed and included three months in the hospital.

After release from the hospital, I was also released from my job as a television broadcast engineer. Another good job was lost that same year. Then my wife said she was leaving me and taking my two little boys. In retrospect this was right where God wanted me, so low I could only look up to Him. In desperation, I joined a home Bible study where I saw life. The couple leading the study was newly reborn in Christ and aglow with the Holy Spirit. God breathed His supernatural life into me. God miraculously healed me of Crohn's disease, gave me custody of my boys, and eventually led me to my wife, Rita, His demonstration to me of amazing grace. I found life.

~~~~~~~~~~~~~~~~~~~~~~~~~~~

We all not only need to be forgiven for our acts of sin. We need to be rescued from our sin nature. God imparts a new nature, His nature, to us.

> *We need forgiveness from what we have done. We need deliverance from what we are.*

Jesus said He is the life. Nothing comes into being or receives life apart from Him. He is our Creator God. He breathed life into us. "He was in the beginning with God. All things came into being through Him (John 1:2–5).

Eternal life is not centered in Heaven. We will enjoy eternal life in Heaven, yet, it [He] is available *now*. Wherever eternal life is mentioned in the New Testament, it is always centered in Christ Jesus. "And the testimony is this, that God has given us eternal life, and this life is in His Son. He who has the Son has the life . . . Jesus Christ, this is the true God and eternal life." (1 John 5:11–12, 20). See also; 1 John 3:15.

Christ is the one who will make Heaven "Heavenly." Jesus is not just the means to the end, Heaven. He is the end, the goal. "For the wages of sin is death, but the free gift of God is eternal life in Christ Jesus our Lord" (Romans 6:23). "…whoever believes will *in Him* have eternal life. For God so loved the world, that He gave His only begotten Son, that whosoever believes *in Him* shall not perish, but have eternal life...He who believes in the Son *has* eternal life" (emphasis mine). Believers have passed out of death into life.

In Jesus' final message before the cross He prayed to the Father, "This is eternal life, that they may know You, the only true God, and Jesus Christ whom You have sent" (John 17:3). We cannot really know a distant God. John lived with Jesus before and after His ascension.

One news reporter I heard thought it amazing that Evangelist Billy Graham claimed to have a "personal relationship with God." Having a personal relationship with the God of the universe *is* an amazing thing. The reporter would probably be astonished that born-again Christians have Christ in them.

I believe much of the lack of life in the church is due to the lack of the knowledge of the indwelling Christ. If He's not in us, it's all up to us. This leads to legalistic self-effort. We ask Him to be with us when He already is. His actual presence is missing, of course, in those who are Christians in name only.

"For we are His workmanship, created in Christ Jesus for good works…" (Ephesians 2:10), but we are not put on Earth to work for Jesus in His stead. If we are working for Jesus, does that mean He is unemployed, or merely our boss? We are here for Him to live in and through us. Martin Luther's great hymn states, "Did we in our own strength confide our striving would be losing." He doesn't give us life apart from Himself. He *is* our life (Colossians 3:4).

God is the doer. He just uses our hands and our feet, our brains and our mouths. We are His body. As Watchman Nee's book title infers, this should be the *Normal Christian Life*. Nee writes:

> Praise the Lord for the reality of
> His life within. But why is there so little

expression of that life? Why is it not overflowing and imparting life to others?...We are living in the soul; we are working and serving in our own natural strength . . . lose it; for that way lies fullness . . . when the soul becomes our life we live as rebels and fugitives from God—gifted, cultured, educated, no doubt, but alienated from the life of God. But when we come to live our life in the Spirit and by the Spirit, though we still use our soul faculties, just as we do our physical faculties, they are now the servants of the Spirit; and when we have reached that point, God can really use us.

Though stated earlier, it bears repeating; Jesus did nothing on Earth by His own initiative. He lived by the life of the Father. Amazingly, in the 21 chapters of the Gospel of John, more than 42 times, Jesus said or inferred He did and said nothing except what the Father told Him. When He repeats Himself that many times, shouldn't we take notice? We are to live by the life of Another also. We are His hands and mouth, but He, the Head, must control and direct the actions of us, His body. A headless body has no life. A beheaded chicken may look like it is alive for a short while. It might run in circles or light out for California, but it will burn out quickly. It has no direction or purpose, other than to be consumed.

So it is with us, apart from Christ our Head.

The "church" in the United States seems to be fast approaching the state of the church in Europe, where there is very little life. Many churches claim to be Bible-believing churches, and yet deny God's power for Christian living. While Jesus gives life to prayer, Bible study, and church attendance, there is no life in them apart from Christ our life. Philippians 1:6 states, "For I am confident of this very thing, that He who began a good work in you will perfect [perform $_{KJV}$] it until the day of Christ Jesus." Life is not in our doing, but in being in Him. Charles Trumbull in *The Life that Wins* wrote:

> There is only one life that wins, and that is the life of Jesus Christ. Every man may have that life; every man may live that life. I do not mean that every man may be Christ-like . . . have Christ's help . . . have power from Christ . . . be merely saved from his sins and kept from sinning; I mean something better than even that victory . . . Jesus Christ was actually and literally within me . . . Christ had constituted Himself my life— not as a figure of speech, remember, but as a literal actual fact . . . my experience is like that of every other man of God . . . first failure, then a sense of need. Thereafter an awareness of the secret

of the indwelling Savior, a secret so simple that most Christians stumble over it or are unaware of it.

In Luke 19:44, Jesus prophecies judgment on the Jews for they "did not recognize the time of your visitation" by the Messiah. As stated in the first chapter, I think most of the church today does not recognize the time of our visitation by the Spirit of Christ. He has given us His authority, power, and indwelling nature (Acts 1:8).

We are the vessels in which He dwells. This makes us vessels of honor, but the real Treasure is within us. "But we have this treasure in earthen vessels, so that the surpassing greatness of the power will be of God and not from ourselves" (2 Corinthians 4:7). We are not meant to merely contain our precious Jesus, but to overflow with Him, out to others. He was broken and spilled out for us, and we must also be broken before others can see Him and not merely the vessel.

D. Thomas Lancaster in *The Mystery of the Gospel* states: "So we recognize three different truths at the same time: that *we* are dead; that He now lives *as* us; but that the union is so complete that we can say *we* live . . . It is He and I acting as one." We are crucified, dead, raised to new life, and ascended with Christ (Ephesians 2:6, Galatians).

Jesus said in John 15:5, if we abide in Him, we will bear much fruit. This living in Him means not trying to find our life in the world, or in a self-centered existence. "Set your mind on the things above, not on the things that are on Earth. For you have died and your life is hidden with Christ in God" (Colossians 3:2–3).

> *Our life must be hidden for His life to be seen.*

Jesus said, "Truly, truly, I say to you, unless a grain of wheat falls into the Earth and dies, it remains alone; but if it dies, it bears much fruit. He who loves his life loses it, and he who hates his life in this world will keep it to life eternal" (John 12:24–25). It is in your dying He lives.

The church has too often focused only on our ticket to Heaven. This is through the finished work of the cross. But there is an ongoing work of the indwelling Christ as well. "If, while we were his enemies, Christ reconciled us to God by dying for us, surely now we are reconciled we may be perfectly certain of our salvation by His living in us" (Romans 5:10, Phillips New Testament).

> *Christ's death on the cross saves us from the wrath of God. His indwelling life saves us from the power of the devil, the world, and our flesh.*

"Not that we are adequate in ourselves to consider anything as coming from ourselves, but our adequacy is from God . . . the Spirit gives life" (2 Corinthians 3:5–6). This is why the Bible says we are complete in Him. Self doesn't need improvement. Self needs to be dead, buried, and resurrected with Him that we might live with and by Him.

Jesus said we are blessed when we hunger and thirst for righteousness (Matthew 5:6). He also said, when we come to Him we will never hunger or thirst (John 6:35). He is the satisfaction of this longing,

Summary of John 14:6

Jesus said, "I am the way, and the truth, and the life; no one comes to the Father but through Me" (John 14:6). We are to seek no other way, truth, or life. Jesus is the way into the presence of the Godhead. He is the embodiment of the truth of God, the very mind of God. Jesus is the eternal life in all He possesses. "In Him was life, and the life was the Light of men" (John 1:4). The way for God to make Himself known to man was to become a man. The only way for Him to make Himself known today is that He be clearly seen in Christians. "For of His fullness we have all received, and grace upon grace" (John 1:11).

What could be better than walking with Jesus on this Earth like His disciples did? Our life with His indwelling Spirit is better, Jesus said (John 14:12 & 16:7). Nevertheless, a better day yet is coming. The Holy Spirit is just a pledge or foretaste of what is to come in Heaven, when we will be "swallowed up by life" (2 Corinthians 5:4). Life is good. Yes, He is.

9. THE WORDS IN BLACK

Simon Peter said to Him, "Lord, where are you going?" (John 13:36)

The words of Jesus in my Bible are in red ink. Our text, John 13:31 through John 17, is mostly in red. The few words in black are mostly questions of Jesus' disciples, indicating their lack of understanding of what He was saying and where He was going. It was clear Jesus could not just say, "You're good to go. See you later."

He said He would give them "another Helper" (John 14:16). He would not leave them as orphans (vs. 18). He would indwell them (vs. 20). He and the Father would make their home with them (vs. 23), to teach them (vs. 26), make them fruitful (15:4), guide them to truth (16:13), and perfect them (17:23). Their and our neediness made the coming of His Holy Spirit so necessary. We need to live by the life of God's Spirit just as Jesus did.

After all this time with Jesus, His disciples still didn't get it, partly because they still lacked the Holy

Spirit, but also Jesus didn't fully reveal how He would fulfill the Law and usher in the New Covenant by His death and resurrection. For instance, Jesus said we must be perfect, but didn't say how (Matthew 5:48). In John 17:23 He says we are perfected in unity with Him. It was the Apostle Paul who explained we are complete or perfect in Christ, perfected in holiness (2 Corinthians 7:1, Colossians 2:9–10, Romans 8:10–11).

Unlike Jesus' disciples, we live this side of the cross and have the New Testament. But do we really understand what He accomplished for us on the cross? Do we live by the life of the indwelling Holy Spirit, as Jesus did? The church is a living organism with Christ as the head, teeming with life.

Let's look at the few comments of the disciples during Jesus' long message.

Peter said, "Lord, where are you going?" Jesus answered, "Where I go, you cannot follow Me now; but you will follow later" (John 13:36). Was Jesus saying Peter would follow Him to the cross? Peter was also crucified later. Was Jesus saying Peter would follow Him to Heaven? This was true also. Or was Jesus saying Peter would be a true follower after Pentecost? Peter would die to self and be filled with the Holy Spirit, seeing greater works, answered prayer, fruitfulness, and the power to truly live by the indwelling life of God? Only the Holy Spirit can answer for us.

However, I think this indicates there are layers of truth in God's Word. For instance, when Jesus said, "I go to prepare a place for you," was He speaking of an eternal dwelling place in Heaven, a place in God for us, or a dwelling place in us for the Holy Spirit? All of these were prepared for us on the cross.

Peter said to Him, "Lord, why can I not follow You right now? I will lay down my life for You." Jesus answered, "Will you lay down your life for Me? Truly, truly, I say to you, a rooster will not crow until you deny Me three times. Do not let your heart be troubled" (John 13:37–14:1). Peter had no power to either live or die for Jesus. Jesus expected nothing of Peter but failure apart from Him. He expects no more of us. But Peter would, and we shall receive power after the Holy Spirit is come upon us, both to live and to die for Christ if necessary. But Christ mainly wants us to be "living sacrifices" serving Him (Romans 12:1).

Jesus said, "And you know the way where I am going." **Thomas said to Him, "Lord, we do not know where You are going, how do we know the way?"** Jesus said to him, "I am the way, and the truth, and the life; no one comes to the Father but through Me" (John 14:4–6). They knew Jesus was the Messiah, but not the kind of Messiah they understood from the prophecies of the Old Testament. When Jesus asked His disciples, "Who do you say that I am?" Simon Peter answered, "You are the Christ, the Son of the living God." Jesus told him his intellect didn't show him this. The Father did (Matthew 16:15–17). The only way they or we can understand the Scriptures is if God reveals it to us.

Jesus said, "But the Helper, the Holy Spirit, whom the Father will send in My name, He will teach you all things, and bring to your remembrance all that I said to you" (John 14:26). I doubt if John took detailed notes of this long message of Jesus, especially when he understood little of it. Years later, the Holy Spirit would bring it to his "remembrance" so he could write this supernaturally given Gospel.

Philip said to Him, "Lord, show us the Father, and it is enough for us." Jesus said to him, "Have I been so long with you, and yet you have not come to know Me, Phillip?" (John 14:8–9). We too may have been Christians for years, and yet, we have not really come to know Him as we should. We may have been too busy serving Him to just sit at His feet to know Him better. They were seeking and needing something more, but it was to be found in the indwelling Spirit of Christ alone. He was with them, but would soon be within them (John 14:17, Acts 1:8).

This raises the question: were they born again at this point? Are not all believers indwelt by the Holy Spirit? Yet, in their case, Jesus points to a future indwelling of the Spirit with power. They still lived under the Old Covenant, where the Holy Spirit was present but not in them until His outpouring at Pentecost. Old Covenant believers could be saved and yet not indwelt by the Spirit.

All the fullness of Deity dwelt in Jesus of

Nazareth, and now He dwells in us, the body of Christ (Colossians 2:9–10). We don't possess Him. He possesses and owns us. As the branch to the vine, so Christ's life flows through us. Grace is just His indwelling unmerited love in action. Just as He who had seen Jesus had seen the Father, so His life should be clearly seen in us.

After Jesus had said He would disclose Himself to them, **Judas (not Iscariot) said to Him, "Lord, what then has happened that You are going to disclose Yourself to us and not to the world?"** Jesus answered, "If anyone loves Me, he will keep My word; and My Father will love him, and We will come to him and make Our abode with him" (John 14:22–23). "We," the Father and the Son, would be living in them and us. Even though the disciples understood so little, He would disclose Himself to them because of their intense love and devotion to Him. Faith comes by hearing, and they kept on listening and following Him.

Older Christians have said to me, "I've never heard these things taught before." They should read the writings of Andrew Murray, A. B. Simpson, and Watchman Nee. Gene Edwards says in *Experiencing The Depths of Jesus Christ:*

> This era . . . the most Bible-centered age since the days of the Pharisees . . . also rivals their age for being the *least* Christ-centered. (And men of today get just as mad as men of that former age

when someone points out the fact. Making Scripture the center of your life instead of Christ always tends to give you a very ornery disposition.) . . . We seem to be more totally blind to our deprivation than all other centuries lumped together.

The title of this book says much. It is the depth of Christ we can experience, not possess. He can possess us and reveal Himself to us, but we own no spiritual depth of our own. It is usually when He brings us to the end of our self we experience the deep things of God.

Many are content with a supposed ticket to Heaven, yet, know little of an indwelling Lord. Jesus spoke of those not knowing Him doing very impressive works as unbelievers (Matthew 7:21–23). Jesus is looking for an intimate relationship with us. Can we miss One so near?

> *He can possess us and reveal Himself to us, but we own no spiritual depth of our own.*

He stands at the door of our hearts knocking, and will come into those hearts that open to Him in a deep desire to know Him more (Revelation 3:20). Sometimes He has to knock louder with the hard knocks of life to get our attention. We can even give thanks for troubles. John Eldredge in *Waking the Dead* writes:

> We begin by assuming that God is still speaking. An old hymn celebrating the wonderful Scriptures (How Firm a Foundation) has a line; 'What more can He say than to you He has said?' The implication is that God has said all He has to say to us in the Bible, period. It sounds orthodox. Except it's not what the Bible says: Jesus said, 'I have much more to say to you, more than you can now bear. But when He, the Spirit of truth comes, He will guide you into all truth' (John 16:12-13) . . . now that His Spirit resides in your heart, the conversation can continue . . . generously, intimately . . . The Religious Spirit has turned discipleship into a soul-killing exercise of principles. Most folks don't even know they can walk with God, hear His voice . . . The result has been a faith stripped of the supernatural, the Christianity of tips and techniques.

Our subjective experience confirms the objective truth of the Bible. For example, 2 Peter 1:16–19 states "we were eyewitnesses of His majesty . . . So we have the prophetic word made more sure."

~~~~~~~~~~~~~~~~~~~~~~~~~~~~~

Jesus also said His sheep hear His voice and follow Him. I too often don't listen enough for His guidance, but let me share an incident when I did. My wife Rita and I were traveling across New York State to a camp where we were volunteering. We had stopped for the night. The next morning it rained. Not wanting to travel in the rain, I vacillated about leaving. I thought, "Well, I can pray about it." Before I prayed, I read a devotion and the words, **move forward**, and **seize the opportunity** practically jumped off the page at me. I said, "Okay Lord." We left in the rain. There had been flooding across the state. We had planned to stay at a campground called Riverside. Rita said, "Duh! We are not staying at a campground with that name." A happy wife is a happy life. When we arrived at our destination, television news reported the interstate highway had washed out behind us, and two tractor-trailer rigs had gone into the water, killing both drivers. God still needs to speak to His children by other means than the Bible.

~~~~~~~~~~~~~~~~~~~~~~~~~~

How can we know He is with us unless He guides, teaches, and counsels us? Never contradicting the Bible, the Holy Spirit speaks to us in many ways; through a still small voice, thoughts that seem to be our own when in fellowship with Him, using circumstances, and people, including pastors and teachers.

Some of His disciples then said to one another, "What is this thing He is telling us, 'A little while, and you will not see Me; and again a little while, and you will see Me'; and, 'because I go to the Father'?" . . . "We do not know what He is talking about." Jesus said, "Truly, truly, I say to you, that you will weep and lament, but the world will rejoice; you will be sorrowful, but your sorrow will be turned to joy" (John 16:17–20). They would have joy after He rose from the dead, at His second coming, and when they experienced His indwelling life.

Of the comments of Jesus' disciples interspersed throughout His message, the sixth and final comment is the only one which was not a question. It was in response to Jesus' statement, "I came forth from the Father and have come into the world; I am leaving the world again and going to the

Father." **His disciples said, "Lo, now You are speaking plainly and are not using a figure of speech. Now we know that You know all things, and have no need for anyone to question You; by this we believe that You came from God."** Jesus answered, "Do you now believe? Behold, an hour is coming and has already come, for you to be scattered, each to his own home, and to leave Me alone" (John 16:29–32).

They said they now believed, but He said their faith would be tested and found wanting. They would receive power, His power, and life after the Holy Spirit would come to indwell them and give them revelation knowledge. This bewildered group of His followers would soon scatter, and if they had not been later filled with the Holy Spirit, we might have no gospel today.

PART II

THE PROMISES OF JESUS

This love letter of Jesus is a message of promise. It is an introduction into a whole new way of living under the New Covenant. We have already looked at Jesus' promise of the Holy Spirit, the indwelling life of God. Out of this all-encompassing promise proceed His other promises in this His last great message to the church. By His indwelling power, He said, will come greater works than He did. The Spirit within us will intercede and we will enjoy answered prayer. His promise of answered prayer and fruitfulness is realized through unity with Him and obedience to Him. And, yes, the servant is not greater than the Master. We are also promised suffering and persecution in following Him.

Not all will experience His promises. He has bought us with His blood. We must bow fully to His lordship. Those who are wholly His will be His holy ones. Too often we want the promises of God without seeking God for Himself. Jeremiah 29:11–13 states:

'For I know the plans that I have for you,' declares the Lord, 'plans for welfare and not for calamity to give you a future and a hope. Then you will call upon Me and come and pray to Me, and I will listen to you. You will seek Me and find Me when you search for Me with all your heart.'

We like the "plans for welfare" part, but sometimes stumble on the "all your heart" part.

The purpose of these promises is we would not just do witnessing, but be witnesses, creating a hunger for Him in those who see His life in us (Acts 1:8).

The assurance of the Holy Spirit with His accompanying fruit and gifts seems like an undeserved indulgence. All this is not for us alone but for a world hungry for the Bread of Life. Let us now examine these promises of our Lord.

10. GREATER WORKS

Do you not believe that I am in the Father, and the Father is in Me? The words that I say to you I do not speak on My own initiative, but the Father abiding in Me does His works. Believe Me that I am in the Father and the Father is in Me; otherwise believe because of the works themselves. Truly, truly, I say to you, he who believes in Me, the works that I do, He will do also; and greater works than these he will do; because I go to the Father. Whatever you ask in My name, that will I do, so that the Father may be glorified in the Son. If you ask Me anything in My name, I will do it (John 14:10–14).

Jesus makes the amazing declaration that His followers would do even greater works than He had. How could we do greater marvels than the Lord Jesus Christ? This seems impossible. But what He once said, remains true today; "What is impossible for man is possible for God" (Luke 18:27).

The key is, Jesus did His works by the power of the Father; "I do not speak on My own initiative, but the Father abiding in Me does His works" (John 14:10). How could Jesus' disciples believe He would be in us if we couldn't believe the Father was in Him? Jesus' humanity limited Him to do and say only what the Father gave Him.

We too can do miraculous works only by His indwelling power. It is not us doing the works, but Him; "that will I do," He said (John 14:13). We can say with the Apostle Paul, "it is no longer I who live, but Christ lives in me" (Galatians 2:20).

Jesus said, "If you ask Me anything in My name, I will do it" (John 14:14). We pray "in Jesus name" often without thinking what it means. In Scripture, a person's name often indicated his nature. Israel means "he persists with God." Immanuel means God with us. To pray in Jesus name is to pray by His power, authority, and indwelling nature. When we ask the Father in His name, the Father sees His Son asking. He indwells us so He can accomplish His purposes through us.

When a woman marries a man, taking his name, it indicates the unity of the relationship. We have no right to use Jesus' name unless we are His bride.

In this same message, (John 15:5) Jesus said, "apart from Me you can do nothing." We can do all kinds of good works *for* God, but Jesus says it is nothing apart from Him. The Bible says in the last days there will be many, "holding to a form of godliness, although they have denied its power" (2 Timothy 3:5). Our only power is in the indwelling Christ. Abiding in Him, we can do anything, even greater wonders than He, for we are not apart from Him. Grace, unmerited favor, means doing the impossible in union with Him. Through the body of Christ, the ministry of Jesus is still operative. Should we go to the doctor for healing, or Him, first?

We still haven't fully answered the question, how could we do *greater* works than Jesus. Did He mean greater in number, or greater in magnitude? I think He meant both. As a man, He could only be in one place at a time, whereas millions of believers through the ages would do innumerable works around the globe.

But I believe Jesus was also saying the works we would do would be greater in magnitude or significance. Let me illustrate: suppose a man in church suddenly had a massive heart attack and dropped dead. The people around him tried to revive him to no avail. After the ambulance had arrived, he was pronounced dead. Then someone said, "Let's pray for a miracle." To everyone's surprise, God raises him from the dead. Seeing this, one of the people comes to saving faith in God. Which is the greater work, the man who is raised from physical death, or the person who is raised from spiritual death? I believe the spiritual awakening was the greater work.

While Jesus raised the dead and healed the sick, the indwelling Holy Spirit was not yet a reality for man under the Old Covenant. But in John 13 through 17, He is introducing the new covenant of supernatural works and greater fruitfulness through the coming of the Spirit to perform what Jesus had made possible. Sin had separated us from God. Now, after Jesus' work on the cross, the Spirit of the Father and the Son would live within us, empowering us for greater works. "Greater is He who is in you, than he who is in the world" (1 John 4:4). If the Christian life and Christ's indwelling of us are supernatural, shouldn't signs and wonders follow?

Spiritual works would be greater wonders than Jesus' physical miracles. After feeding the five thousand, the people were following Jesus just for what He could do for them physically and wanted to do these works themselves (John 6:26–29). Satan's temptation to man has always been that we might be as God.

Jesus' reply in John 6 denoted two important truths. First, only God can do the works of God. Jesus' disciples were promised wonders of God by Him working through them. Second, all of God's works are centered in one work, to bring us to saving faith in Him.

> *If the Christian life and Christ's indwelling of us are supernatural, shouldn't signs and wonders follow?*

Is the physical or the spiritual world the real world to you? Is your daily bread food on the table or Jesus, the bread of life? William Law's early writings were quite legalistic until his grace awakening. He then in *God's Best Secrets* emphasized:

> The only thing that is available for us to rise out of our fallen state and become as we were at creation . . . is the renewal of the original life and power of the Spirit of God in us. Everything else . . . is dead and helpless unless it has the Spirit of God breathing in it . . . divine goodness and virtue in us is nothing but the goodness of God manifesting itself . . . [Jesus' disciples] could not have the Holy Spirit as their Guide until Christ's outward teaching was changed into the inspiration and operation of His Spirit in their souls.

"For it is God who is at work in you, both to will and to work for His good pleasure" (Philippians 2:13).

It is so important to see these four and a half chapters, John 13–17, as one single message of Jesus to understand it in context. The following verses illustrate or infer greater works. Jesus said, "If you loved Me, you would have rejoiced because I go to the Father, for the Father is greater than I" (John 14:28). "...and We will come to him and make Our abode with him" (14:23). "If you abide in Me, and My words abide in you, ask whatever you wish, and it will be done for you" (15:7). "if I do not go away, the Helper will not come to you" (16:7–8). "that they may all be one; even as You, Father, are in Me and I in You, that they also may be in Us" (17:21). "....I in them and You in Me, that they may be perfected in unity, so that the world may know that You sent Me, and loved them, even as You have loved Me" (17:21, 23).

Jesus sent us His Holy Spirit to indwell us "so that the life of Jesus also may be manifested in our mortal flesh" (2 Corinthians 4:11) so we might do amazing works. The life of the One apparent in the many resulted in more remarkable works than the One could do alone.

"Now to Him who is able to do exceeding abundantly beyond all that we could ask or think, according to the power that works within us, to Him be the glory" (Ephesians 3:20–21).

11. ANSWERED PRAYER

Whatever you ask in My name, that will I do, so that the Father may be glorified in the Son. If you ask Me anything in My name, I will do it (John 14:13–14).

Closely related to Jesus' promise of greater works is His pledge of answered prayer. My Bible has the words of Jesus printed in red. While the entire Bible is the inspired word of God, we take special note when the words are the actual words of our Savior. We should really sit up and take notice when Jesus repeats Himself. In this passage of Scripture, John chapters 14–17, Jesus promises us answers to our prayers *seven* times. Obviously, it is a high priority with Him that we receive what we ask from Him.

Also, prayer is about having a vital relationship with our Lord and Friend, an attitude of dependence on Him. Prayer is a continuing conversation with Him that should involve more listening than talking since He already knows what we are going to say. What He has to say is more important.

Jesus' goal in these answers is, "that the Father may be glorified in the Son" (John 14:13). The Son is the glory and expression of all the Father is. When our prayers are answered, it expresses the glory of God.

~~~~~~~~~~~~~~~~~~~~~~~~~~~~~~~

My wife, Rita, and I try to pray before trips. While pulling our fifth-wheel RV through Arkansas our truck's engine suddenly died. As I eased the truck to the shoulder of the road, I saw another truck pulling over behind me. God positioned a man who delivered RVs for a living right behind us. He towed us, asking for no payment. God knows where we live, even when we keep moving.

~~~~~~~~~~~~~~~~~~~~~~~~~~~~~~~

In John 15:7 Jesus promises, "If you abide in Me, and My words abide in you, ask whatever you wish, and it will be done for you. By this is My Father glorified, that you bear much fruit, and so prove to be My disciples." Fruitfulness is encompassed in the love of the Holy Spirit. It is the expression of the glory of God in and through us.

This goal of fruitfulness in answer to prayer is also mentioned in Jesus' promise in John 15:16. We should be asking God how we can bless Him, rather than only asking Him to bless us.

Unbelief or self-sufficiency often fuels self-indulgence. "You do not have because you do not ask. You ask and you do not receive, because you ask with wrong motives, so that you may spend it on your pleasures" (James 4:2–3).

> *The fruit of the Spirit is food for a hungry world.*

In John 16:24 Jesus promises, "Until now you have asked for nothing in My name; ask and you will receive, so that your joy may be made full." Our joyfulness seems rather self-serving until we realize when the world sees this fruit of the Spirit in us, it creates a hunger in them for this indwelling God who is our life.

At first glance, when Jesus says, "If you ask Me anything in My name, I will do it," it sounds rather open-ended and unconditional. However, He says we must ask *in His name.* This is by His authority, power, and indwelling nature.

This condition for answered prayer is expressed differently in John 15:7; "If you abide [stay] in Me, and My words abide in you, ask whatever you wish, and it will be done for you." If our minds and hearts are stayed on Jesus, we may ask whatever we wish, for it will be the will of God. Those who abide in

Christ are not self-centered; they "have the mind of Christ" (1 Corinthians 2:16).

Being rightly related to God we can expect answers to prayer. Psalm 37:4 states, "Delight yourself in the Lord; and He will give you the desires of your heart." I love this Scripture because it so wonderfully illustrates layers of truth in the Bible. What I mean by "layers," is as we grow in the Lord He reveals more and more truth from the same verses. The Scripture begins to blossom and bloom with newfound beauty.

As new Christians, we are delighted Psalm 37 seems to promise us anything we desire. As we grow to love Him more, we come to see when we delight in Him, then *He Himself* is the desire of our heart. Our desire is to know Him more. As we grow in grace, we may see yet another dimension to this verse. *"He will give you"* the desires of your heart. The desires will come from Him. Out of a close relationship with Jesus will come a unity of purpose and desire. Sometimes we wonder, *was that His thought or mine?* While we are here for God's pleasure, He sure delights to delight us.

~~~~~~~~~~~~~~~~~~~~~~~~~~~~

When author Catherine Marshall and her husband, Peter, former chaplain of the U. S. Senate, were dating, Catherine expressed her desire to marry him. She quickly apologized. Peter told her not to be embarrassed.

He said when we are in close intimacy
with the Lord "His thoughts and
desires become ours, and ours become
His."

~~~~~~~~~~~~~~~~~~~~~~~~~~~

We can be confident of answered prayer when
we ask anything according to His will (1 John 5:14–
15). He will share more and more with us as we get
to know Him better. What better way than to pray?
V. Raymond Edman in *They Found the Secret* shares
his experience with a man called Praying Hyde:

> At one of our missions in
> England the audience was extremely
> small, results seemed impossible but I
> received a note saying that an American
> missionary was coming to the town and
> was going to pray God's blessing upon
> our work. He was known as 'Praying
> Hyde.' Almost instantly the tide turned.
> The hall was packed, and my first
> invitation meant fifty men for Jesus
> Christ. As we were leaving I said, 'Mr.
> Hyde, I want you to pray for me.' He
> came to my room, turned the key in the
> door, dropped on his knees, waited five
> minutes without a single syllable
> coming from his lips. I could hear my
> heart thumping and beating. I felt the
> hot tears running down my face. I

knew I was with God. Then with upturned face, down which the tears were streaming, he said: 'Oh, God!' Then for five minutes at least, he was still again, and then when he knew he was walking with God his arm went around my shoulder and there came up from the depth of his heart such petitions for men as I had never heard before. I rose from my knees to know what real prayer was . . .

I heard one zealous young man exclaim, "If you want to be heard by God, you have to squall and bawl and blow snot." While it is good to be fervent in prayer, I believe God hears even a silent tear. He knows our hearts.

> *When Jesus is our heart's desire,*
> *His desires become ours.*

Jesus taught us how to pray. He said we should go to a quiet place alone with our "Father who is in secret." We should not use "meaningless repetition" but short prayers, since "your Father knows what you need before you ask Him" (Matthew 6:6–8). I just noticed it says our Father "is in secret." He isn't standing out in the open, but hidden in a quiet place, bidding us to get alone with Him where we won't be tempted to impress others with our prayers. Some seem to think if we say a short prayer, others will think we are not very spiritual.

~~~~~~~~~~~~~~~~~~~~~~~~~

One Summer I flew to Boston and then took a bus to Maine to visit our son and his family. On the return trip, when I boarded the bus, the driver quickly informed me I would not make it to the airport in time for my flight. Normally I would have started my wheels turning to figure what to do next. But God's peace quickly settled on me and I just rested in Him, a very pleasant place. When I finally arrived at the airport, I was quickly informed my plane had been delayed, so I was right on time! If I were more a man of faith, I wouldn't have put that exclamation point there. We should expect answered prayer, even when prayer is unspoken.

~~~~~~~~~~~~~~~~~~~~~~~~~

Having died for us, answering our prayers seems trivial in comparison. "He who did not spare His own Son, but delivered Him over for us all, how will He not also with Him freely give us all things?" (Romans 8:32). We often fall short in exercising this great privilege of prayer. We are often too self-sufficient. If Jesus relied so completely on His Heavenly Father for all things, what makes us think we can be anything but dysfunctional apart from Him?

After Jesus emphasized His desire to answer prayer in John 14–17, He then demonstrates the importance of dependent prayer, with His high priestly prayer to the Father in chapter seventeen.

The evil one desires to separate us from God and each other. In John 17:11–17 Jesus prayed, "Holy Father, keep them in Your name, the name which You have given Me, that they may be one even as We are . . . that they may have My joy made full in themselves . . . I do not ask You to take them out of the world, but to keep them from the evil one . . . Sanctify them in the truth; Your word is truth." To be in context with the rest of this message of Jesus, He must have been referring to Himself as the word, not the Scriptures. He is both the truth and the sanctifier.

He asks the Father to set us apart in unity with the Godhead and each other. We being "perfected in unity" seems to sum up Jesus' last message before the cross. "I have made Your name known to them, and will make it known, so that the love wherewith You have loved Me may be in them, and I in them" (17:26).

In studying this passage of Scripture on prayer, I see three goals of Jesus:

1. God would be glorified.
2. Our joy would be full.

3. The world may know who He is.
Stated another way; God will be glorified when our joy is made full for the world to see and be drawn to Jesus.

St. Francis once said: "Preach Jesus always, even if you have to use words."

12. THE COMMANDMENTS KEPT

If anyone loves Me, he will keep My word
(John 14:23).

In the last two chapters we looked at Jesus' promises, we would do greater works than He, and our prayers would be answered. Let's look at His promise that we will keep His commandments. That's right, promise. The commands of the Old Covenant said, "You must," the New Covenant affirms, "You will." What God commanded He now makes possible. "For sin shall not be master over you, for you are not under law but under grace" (Romans 6:14). "No one who is born of God practices sin" (1 John 3:9). The Law gave no power to keep it. With Jesus' commandments comes the power of the Spirit to keep them.

> *The commandments of the Old Covenant have become the promises of the New Covenant.*

Jesus promised us answered prayers *seven times* in this message before the cross. He also emphasized His commandments *nine times* in this message. How important could this be?

Many of us have struggled or even given up on keeping Jesus' two commandments; to love the Lord with *all* our hearts and to love others *as* our selves. He also said we must be perfect, which is not natural to our human nature. Yet He has given Christians a supernatural nature. We should give up trying in our own power and trust more in God's indwelling Spirit. The Father commanded obedience. Jesus died for our disobedience. The Holy Spirit imparts His perfection in us. Jesus said we are perfected in unity with him.

L. E. Maxwell in *Born Crucified* states:

> He [Jesus] was continually bringing man face to face with the impossible. He laid upon men commands which were utterly contrary to the flesh and to human understanding . . . that human nature love its enemies, turn the other cheek, rejoice in suffering, in reproach, in persecution . . . And what was all this

for but to bring men face to face with themselves, with Deity, and with their need of His grace to do these very impossibles.

In our text, three times Jesus gives us His commandment that we love one another (John 13:34, 15:12, 15:17). Jesus shows when we love Him we will also love one another. "He who has My commandments and keeps them is the one who loves Me" (14:21). "If anyone loves Me, he will keep My word" (14:23). He does not say "should" but "will". What is love but fruit of the Spirit?

You might say no person ever kept the commandments perfectly. One did, the man Christ Jesus. He did, and still does, and He lives within us to do what we cannot. "For the mind set on the flesh is death, but the mind set on the Spirit is life and peace" We cannot please God by mere self-effort. However, by His indwelling Spirit, righteousness is clearly evident in our lives (Romans 8:6–11).

We will not be judged so much for works we have done, but for what we have done with Jesus. Have we trusted His work on the cross as well as His work within us? We are not able in ourselves, but He is our ability and our life. "For the gospel has for this reason been preached even to those who are dead, that though they are judged in the flesh as men, they may live in the Spirit according to the will of God"

(1 Peter 4:6). We were dead in our sins, but are now alive in Him.

> *We will not be judged so much for works we have done, but for what we have done with Jesus.*

Since God is love, love fulfills the Law. "For Christ is the end of the law for righteousness to everyone who believes" (Romans 10:4). "End" here means goal or fulfillment, since Jesus said He did not come to do away with the Law but to fulfill it. In *The Mystery of The Gospel* by D. Thomas Lancaster we read:

> The striving of man to "be better" is just the manifestation of self . . . Some ministers stress living righteously, but it is based on self-effort – obedience to the right laws or principles – instead of on the natural, spontaneous flow of the inner life of Christ.

Too often we get the cart before the horse, thinking if we just keep God's commandments, we attain to eternal life. This is trying to be something we are not. We must first be indwelt by God in order to be righteous. Being a Christian is supernatural. He didn't overhaul us but made us new creations. What a glorious miracle when others see Him in us. Think of the wonderful difference between growing "in the grace and knowledge of our Lord and Savior Jesus Christ" (2 Peter 3:18) and growing by self-improvement. Don Anderson in *God Wants A Relationship, Not A Performance* states:

> If there is one misconception that can be singled out as the major cause of breakdown in the Christian life, it's the idea that a human being is capable of performing to please God. The desire to do just that infects the saved and the unsaved.

Satan has subtle ways of perverting the truth. The WWJD (what would Jesus do?) movement is an example. It sounds good. In any situation just ask yourself, "What would Jesus do if He were here and involved in this situation?" Well, He is here and involved with you. But the real danger is someone who is not born again might just try to live by this motto. We *must* be born again. Christ in us is our only hope. Imitation is not the answer. This was Satan's deception to Adam and Eve, "You shall be like God." We must be inhabited by God. Why settle for an imitation when the real Jesus lives within us?

> *The new nature needs no improvement because it is His nature.*

We are complete in Him, lacking nothing (Colossians 2:10). Growing in the grace and knowledge of our Lord is learning to trust Him as our all in all, our perfection. Does this not require some effort? Yes, trusting Him, not our best efforts. "that we may present every man complete in Christ. For this purpose also I labor, striving according to His power, which mightily works within me" (Colossians 1:28–29).

Blaise Pascal in *Foundations of the Christian Religion* states: "It is equally dangerous for man to know God without knowing his own wretchedness, and to know his own wretchedness without knowing the Redeemer who can free him from it."

> *If we were capable of performing to please God, Jesus would not have had to die for our sinful nature.*

I thought, *Isn't God pleased when we are loving?* If we love, it is the fruit *of the Spirit,* not our own fruit. Yet, in so many churches you will be given tips, techniques, and spiritual principles (Biblical, mind you) to get your flesh to behave. Hebrews 5 and 6 refers to these as elementary education. We need to move on to maturity in Christ. Popular contemporary author John Eldredge in *Waking the Dead* writes:

> Christians have spent their lives mastering all sorts of principles, done their duty, and carried on the programs of their church . . . and never known God intimately, heart to heart. There is that troubling passage Jesus gives . . . 'Many will say to Me on that day', "Lord, Lord, did we not" do all sorts of Christian things, amazing things? And Christ will say, 'I never knew you'" (Matthew 7:22–23).

Jesus is looking for a love relationship with us, not a performance. Out of His indwelling love will flow love, which is all He commanded from the beginning. Even though David, Mary Magdalene, and Peter didn't measure up in their performances, they got that one thing right, *love* for their Savior.

We might at first see God's love being conditioned on us keeping Jesus' commandments; "If you keep My commandments, you will abide in

My love" (John 15:10). But read the rest of the verse: "just as I have kept My Father's commandments and abide in His love." Jesus' abiding in the love of the Father resulted in the keeping of the Father's will, so it is with us. Classic devotional writer Oswald Chambers in *My Utmost for His Highest* states:

> Jesus Christ did not come to *teach* only; He came to m*ake me what He teaches I should be.* The Redemption means that Jesus Christ can put into any man the disposition that ruled His own life, and all the standards God gives are based on that disposition . . . Sanctification is not something Jesus Christ puts into me: it is Himself in me . . . The one marvelous secret of a holy life lies not in imitating Jesus, but in letting the perfections of Jesus manifest themselves in my mortal flesh. Sanctification is 'Christ in you.

The purpose of the Law shows how we can be complete in Christ. The Law was given to make man see his sin and turn to God, "because by the works of the Law no flesh will be justified in His sight; for through the Law comes the knowledge of sin" (Romans 3:20). This is why the Law is called a "ministry of death" and "condemnation" (2 Corinthians 3:7–9). The Law condemns us to death for our sin and is meant to turn us to God for salvation. The Law is replaced by "the law of the Spirit of life in Christ" for those who walk by the Spirit (Romans 8:1–4).

The Law is fulfilled in us, by the Holy Spirit of Christ in us (Romans 5:5). Since God is love, and God indwells us, His loving in and through us is the keeping of the commandments of Jesus. We have everything we need in Him.

Only one thing is required – love. St. Augustine said, "Love, then do what you please." There is a lot of truth in that statement. If we live in the love of God, doing what we please will please God.

Paul said, "But we have the mind of Christ" (1 Corinthians 2:16). If His mind is in us, we can expect His desires, love, and righteousness will become ours. "But by His doing you are in Christ Jesus, who *became* to us wisdom from God, and righteousness and sanctification, and redemption" (1 Corinthians 1:30, emphasis mine). 1 John 4:17 the Phillips Translation reads, "Our life in this world is actually His life lived in us." He gives us no spiritual life apart from Himself. Jesus is the indwelling Word of God.

Just as Christ is both in Heaven and in us, so are we both "seated with Him in the Heavenly places" (Ephesians 2:6) and living in Him here on Earth. Christ's presence will make Heaven Heavenly, just as His presence in us can be Heavenly. His presence with us makes us citizens of the Heavenly realm. "For you have died and your life is hidden with Christ in God. When Christ, *who is our life*, is revealed, then you also will be revealed with Him in glory" (Colossians 3:2–3) [emphasis mine]. The Law reveals the character of God. He desires to manifest that life in and through us. His Spirit fulfills the Law in us.

> *Christ's presence will make Heaven heavenly, just as His presence in us can be heavenly.*

Consecration, dedication, and commitment are no substitute for the indwelling life of Christ. With God's Spirit comes the ability to obey. Ezekiel also foretells the new life available to us in Christ.

> Moreover, *I will* give you a new heart and put a new spirit within you; and *I will* remove the heart of stone from your flesh and give you a heart of flesh. *I will* put My Spirit within you and *cause* you to walk in My statutes, and *you will* be careful to observe My ordinances (Ezekiel 36:26–27) [emphasis mine].

When Jesus told the woman at the well to "go and sin no more," He didn't expect her to just pull herself up by her bootstraps (or sandal straps) and do her best to sin no more. When He spoke to her,

He spoke words of life to her. He gave her the "living water" of the Holy Spirit. Hopefully, she received Him.

We are to "glory in Christ Jesus and put no confidence in the flesh" (Philippians 3:3). Love comes out of the life Jesus is. When we love, it is Jesus manifesting Himself through us to others. Apart from Him we really can do nothing of worth. "For to me, to live is Christ and to die is gain" (Philippians 1:21). For me also, to love is Christ, and to die to self daily that His will would be done in me is gain. To see Him come forth is a very sweet death.

God wants us to experience abundant life, not just for our own enjoyment, but so others might hunger for this life they see in us.

"The one who keeps His commandments abides in Him, and He in him" (1 John 3:24). This does not mean sinless perfection. Our old sin nature is not eradicated, but we do receive a new nature, Christ's nature. Indeed, all of Jesus' promises in this message (greater works, answered prayer, fruitfulness, and obedience to His commands) are fulfilled by the overshadowing promise of the indwelling Spirit of God.

13. FRUITFULNESS

I am the vine, you are the branches; he who abides in Me and I in him, he bears much fruit, for apart from Me you can do nothing (John 15:5).

In addition to the promises of Jesus—of greater works, answered prayer, and the keeping of His commandments— there is also a great guarantee of fruitfulness. These promises are dependent on the overriding promise of His indwelling life. Indeed this pledge is closely intertwined like a fruitful vine with the others. Greater works and fruitfulness cannot be separated. Jesus knew that living in Him, we would be praying for more fruitfulness, including love, joy, patience, kindness, goodness, faithfulness, gentleness, and self–control, so He promised answers to these prayers. The fruit of love is the keeping of God's commandments.

Jesus told His disciples, "This is My commandment, that you love one another, just as I have loved you. Greater love has no one than this that one lay down his life for his friends" (John 15:12–13). Jesus was about to lay down His life in love for us all. Peter vowed he would lay down his life for Jesus. He was not able to do so in the power of the flesh, but after the coming of the Spirit to empower him, he then did give his life for Christ in ministry and in martyrdom. We love because God first loved us and put His love within us.

We are not all called to martyrdom, but to live in love, dying to self-will in order to live by the life of Another. Jesus said, "Truly, truly, I say to you, unless a grain of wheat falls into the Earth and dies, it remains alone; but if it dies, it bears much fruit" (John 12:24). Jesus laid down His life for thirty-three years to do the will of the Father, before going to the cross. After His greater love comes to dwell within us, we are empowered to do glorious works.

> *We were designed to live by the life of Another just as Jesus did.*

Wonderful books have been written about finding life in the Vine, Christ Jesus. Christian's eyes have been opened to the deeper life by abiding in Christ. This life has been referred to as; the life that wins, exchanged life, Spirit-filled life, victorious life, normal Christian life, indwelling life, and the life of grace.

There seems to be a very typical pattern. Many of the classic Christian authors and great preachers have found the abiding life of fruitfulness, they testify, usually after years of serving the Lord mostly in the power of the flesh. D. L. Moody, George Mueller, Hudson Taylor, F. B. Meyer, Andrew Murray, Francis Havergal, Praying Hyde, Ruth Paxson, Amy Carmichael, and others found the secret of abiding in Christ. V. Raymond Edman, president of Wheaton College for over 20 years shares in *They Found the Secret:*

> The deep dealing of God with His children varies in detail but the general pattern seems much alike for individual cases. Into each life there arises an awareness of failure, a falling short of all that one should be in the Lord; then there is a definite meeting with the risen Savior in utter surrender of heart, which is indeed death to self. There follows an appropriation by faith of His resurrection life through the abiding presence of the Holy Spirit.

> *When life is hard, we can just give up, or we can give up and let Jesus take over.*

We must see our neediness. We are so self-sufficient financially, religiously, and spiritually – or so we often think.

We must all come to this central truth, *apart from Jesus we can do nothing.* This does not mean apart from His assistance. He is not our assistant, but our Life. This is why He prayed to the Father, "I in them and You in Me, that they may be perfected in unity" (John 17:23).

In John 15:4 Jesus states, "Abide in Me, and I in you. As the branch cannot bear fruit of itself unless it abides in the vine, so neither can you unless you abide in Me." To abide means to live and remain as one living spiritual organism with Him. There is no fruit, strength, life or holiness apart from Him. He is our all in all. The branches, leaves, fruit, are the expression of the life of the vine, Christ Jesus.

I'm sure you will agree Jesus is present *in* our lives. Yet, do you see He *is* your life? "When Christ who is our life is revealed, then you also will be revealed with Him in glory" (Colossians 3:4). I believe this speaks not only of Christ's glory at His return, but His glorious fruitful presence revealed through us.

> *Christ is not our assistant,*
> *but our life.*

What is the fruit Jesus says we will bear? In this passage of Scripture, John 13 through 17, Jesus mentions three kinds of fruit; peace, joy, and love. Jesus said, "Peace I leave with you; My peace I give to you; not as the world gives do I give to you. Do not let your heart be troubled, nor let it be fearful" (John 14:27). In the world, war must cease, troubles or sickness must end, for there to be peace. But Jesus promises peace in the midst of the storm.

The world will have no peace until the Prince of Peace returns. Yet, Christians have both the Prince and His peace in our hearts. In His presence is peace and rest. The more we learn to abide and rest in Him, the less circumstances will matter to us. "The steadfast of mind You will keep in perfect peace, because he trusts in You" (Isaiah 26:3).

A very over-burdened pastor received a call to visit an elderly lady. While visiting, the lady noticed the strain on his face and lack of peace. She pointed out a picture on the wall of Daniel in the lion's den. She said, "Look closely at Daniel's face. Notice his peaceful countenance. That's because Daniel is not looking at the lions, he is looking up to the Lord."

Jesus was asleep in a boat in the midst of a storm at sea. His disciples cringed in fear because they were looking at the storm instead of Him. The greatest trials can seem insignificant when we keep our eyes and hearts fixed on the Lord. "He is our peace" (Ephesians 2:14).

Again in John 16:32–33, Jesus tells His disciples to take courage even in tribulation. He said peace would flood their souls while resting in Him.

Another fruit of the Spirit Jesus promises us when abiding in Him is joy. "These things I have spoken to you so that My joy may be in you, and that your joy may be made full" (John 15:11). "A little while, and you will not see Me, and again a little while and you will see Me. Truly, truly, I say to you, that you will weep and lament, but the world will rejoice; you will be sorrowful, but your sorrow will be turned to joy...Until now you have asked for nothing in My name; ask and you will receive, so that your joy may be made full" (John 16:19–24). Again in John 17:13 Jesus prays to His Father, "But now I come to You; and these things I speak in the world so that they may have My joy made full in themselves."

Author William Law states in *The Power of the Spirit*: "Man's misery and blindness lies in this, that he has lost the knowledge of God as essentially living within him."

Doesn't it seem this abundant life Jesus promises us of peace and joy is a little indulgent? Does He just want us to enjoy life, with no performance required? The answer, of course, is the joy, peace, and love are not just meant for us alone, but to be seen and desired by the world. For Jesus also asks in His prayer, "I do not ask on behalf of these alone, but for those also who believe in Me through their word" (John 17:20). They must see Christ in us.

Jesus also promises us the fruit of love. "We

love because He first loved us" (1 John 4:19). We had no capacity to love until He came to live within us, for it is the fruit *of the Spirit,* not our fruit. In *God's Best Secrets,* author William Law states:

> Until this birth of the spirit of divine love is found in you, you cannot know what divine love is. Divine love is perfect peace and joy, a freedom from all disquiet, making everything to rejoice in it. It is the Christ of God…the restorer of every lost perfection; a redeemer from all evil; a fulfiller of all righteousness; and a *'peace of God which surpasses all understanding'.*

In the little church I grew up attending, the benediction was, "Now may the peace of God which surpasses all understanding keep your hearts and minds in Christ Jesus our Savior." I liked hearing that since it meant church was over. Then at the age of 39, I was born again. Suddenly I thought, *Wow! Now I have that peace.* In spite of the storms in my life, I was at rest in Jesus.

Love is what Jesus commands, and love is what His Spirit supplies. He said, "He who has My commandments and keeps them is the one who loves Me; and he who loves Me will be loved by My Father, and I will love him and will disclose Myself to him" (John 14:21). Much could be written on the many ways Jesus discloses Himself to us. Paul prayed the life of Christ would be clearly apparent in us (2 Corinthians 4:10–11). I believe he was speaking of the fruit of the Holy Spirit, which might be called facets of His nature.

> *Love is what Jesus commands, and love is what His Spirit supplies.*

Jesus said, "By this is My Father glorified, that you bear much fruit, and so prove to be My disciples. Just as the Father has loved Me, I have also loved you; abide in My love. If you keep My commandments, you will abide in My love; just as I have kept My Father's commandments and abide in His love" (John 15:8–10).

Love proves we are His. We don't need to prove it to Him. The love, joy, and peace He manifests through us are proof to the world we belong to the Lord. Watchman Nee said "God doesn't put us on Earth primarily to teach, preach, or witness. He puts us here to create a hunger in the world for this life they see in us, this love, joy, and peace." Being witnesses is more important than doing witnessing. Yet, the fruitfulness will create a desire in others to hear our testimony. Just as the Apostle Paul said God "was pleased to reveal His Son in me," so Christ needs to be revealed in us to a needy world.

> *The fruit of the Spirit can be called facets of Christ's nature.*

We must be hidden for Christ to be seen. "For you have died and your life is hidden with Christ in God. When Christ who is our life, is revealed, then you also will be revealed with Him in glory" (Colossians 3:3–4). He is to be revealed in us here on Earth, as well as at His second coming. Christ *is* our life. There is no need of waiting until the afterlife to enjoy the supernatural love, joy, and peace that surpasses our human understanding.

14. PERSECUTION

If you were of the world, the world would love its own; but because you are not of the world, but I chose you out of the world, because of this the world hates you. Remember the word that I said to you, "A slave is not greater than his master." If they persecuted Me, they will also persecute you; if they kept My word, they will keep yours also (John 15:19–20).

We love all the other promises in this last message of Jesus before the cross. His promise of persecution is not so easy to receive. Peter said he would die for Jesus. Then the persecution started. Many disciples fled, including Peter. Our own dedication and commitment won't keep us in times of trials. We need the Savior, not just a belief in what He did, but His ever-present indwelling, an assurance He will keep us.

Paul wrote, "But you followed my teaching, conduct, purpose, faith, patience, love, perseverance, persecutions, and suffering, such as happened to me . . . and out of them all the Lord rescued me. Indeed, all who desire to live godly in Christ Jesus will be persecuted" (2 Timothy 3:10–12). Notice the two "alls"; *all* those in Christ will be persecuted. Out of *all* trials, He will rescue us.

We need to be "fixing our eyes on Jesus, the author and perfecter of faith, who for the joy set before Him endured the cross, despising the shame, and has sat down at the right hand of the throne of God" (Hebrews 12:2). Jesus sat down because "It is finished." God rested on the seventh day of *creation*, not because He was tired, but because His creation was completed. Jesus sat down because His work of *re-creation* was finished. We become new creations by faith in His finished work on the cross and rest in His Holy Spirit completing us. Righteousness is both imputed and imparted to us.

When we understand the rest of the Gospel, we will find rest in the Gospel. We can rest in Christ's finished work on the cross and His ongoing work within us. Too often faith is a struggle because we don't trust Him who began a good work in us to complete it. Faith is not in trying but trusting, not in struggling but resting.

> *Righteousness is both imputed and imparted to us.*

When trials cause us to come up short in our prayer life, the Holy Spirit intercedes for us. When we fail in reading the Word, the living Word speaks rest to our souls. The faithful One is enough when our faith is not enough. We always come up short in our flesh. Give up and let God's Spirit take over. We can rest in His unchanging grace.

> *Faith is not in trying but trusting, not in running but resting.*

With the eyes of our faith fixed on Jesus, we will have peace, not as the world gives peace, (John 14:27) after the trouble passes. We can have peace in the midst of the storms and trials of life. Trials will come with or without Jesus, but in Him is peace, rest, and joy in the midst of pain and mistreatment.

> *When we understand the rest of the Gospel, we will find rest in the Gospel.*

Why must we endure these trials and persecutions? We live in a fallen world, and the enemy of our souls seeks to destroy us. Like Job, God gives Satan some leeway to test us. Troubles keep us dependent on God deepening and perfecting our faith. Jesus said, "in Me you may have peace. In the world you have tribulation, but take courage; I have overcome the world" (John 16:33). He has called us out of the darkness of the world into the light of His wonderful presence. We are seated with Him in the Heavenly spiritual realm (Ephesians 2:6). We can have amazing peace as the wars rage around us.

Where will persecution come from? Those of us who have unsaved or unsanctified loved ones know our families can often be our greatest burdens. This is one source of spiritual warfare. "For everyone who does evil hates the Light, and does not come to the Light for fear that his deeds will be exposed" (John 3:20). Those closest to us can hurt us the most, even when that is not their intention. Jesus said, "A man's enemies will be the members of his household . . . And he who does not take up his cross and follow after Me is not worthy of Me. He who has found his life will lose it, and he who has lost his life for My sake will find it" (Matthew 10:36–39). When we die to self to live by the life of Another, it is then we find life indeed, Christ living in us. (Galatians 2:20). We then find the life we once lived was only death dressed in deceptive clothing.

Author L. E. Maxwell in *Born Crucified* states: "Christ did not come to straighten out the natural [human nature], but to "cross" it out . . . God is only our God by a birth of His own divine nature within us."

> *The life we once lived was only death dressed in deceptive clothing.*

Satan is out to divide and conquer. This is why Jesus prayed, "I am no more in the world; and yet they themselves are in the world, and I come to you. Holy Father, keep them in your name, the name which you have given Me, that they may be one even as We are" (John 17:11). We see in His prayer, unity with Him and each other is our salvation from divisions. He continues in verse 15, "I do not ask you to take them out of the world, but to keep them from the evil one." Jesus told Peter that Satan would test him, but He would be praying for Peter. He prays for us also. Greater still, He has not left us alone. He has sent His Holy Spirit to be our strength and keeper.

Persecution will also come from the religious crowd. Jesus promised, "They will make you outcasts . . . because they have not known the Father or Me" (John 16:2–3). Those who seem to know their Bibles but do not know God will defend their own brand of religion tenaciously. Paul wrote that in the last days there would be those "holding to a form of godliness, although they have denied its power" (2 Timothy 3:5). The power of godliness is an indwelling God. Those who try to live by the law or by Christian principles, rather than by the life of God, are the worst persecutors. There is very little love in pious legalists.

> *The power of godliness is an indwelling God.*

The religious leaders had Jesus crucified. The religious crowd is the source of much of the persecution of the last day's church. When the Lord called me to ministry, this is the verse He used; "a wide door for effective service has opened to me, and there are many adversaries" (1 Corinthians 16:9). The Apostle Paul encountered opposition from legalists. So have I. Those who have found their life in Christ alone know what I am talking about. Jesus suffered "outside the camp." We too will be rejected by some of those who call themselves the church, and must suffer with Him outside the camp. If we have never been persecuted as Christians, maybe we should ask if we are in the wrong camp. Authors Dan Stone and Greg Smith share in *The Rest of the Gospel:*

We have to fail. God couldn't be God and let us succeed in the flesh, or we would never know Spirit life. We have the Spirit— we do contain the living God—but if we don't live out of Him, in our daily experience it's like we don't have Him in us at all. Our failures at living the Christian life press us into knowing Him as our Life.

Persecutions and failings are not to be feared. They are a confirmation of in Whom we stand. "The Lord will rescue me from every evil deed, and will bring me safely to His Heavenly kingdom; to Him be the glory forever and ever. Amen" (2 Timothy 4:18).

15. METAMORPHOSIS

Therefore if anyone is in Christ, he is a new creature; the old things passed away; behold, new things have come (2 Corinthians 5:17).

Sometimes I have made the statement that at our age if we sit too long rigor mortis will set in. While visiting with my mother-in-law, she said, "We better get moving, or metamorphosis will set in." We had a good laugh, but I thought about the contrast between the process of death, rigor mortis, and this process of life, metamorphosis. I thought. *That's it! My last chapter for this book.*

An example of metamorphosis is a caterpillar becoming a butterfly. This is comparable to when we are born again. We are transformed, transfigured if you will, and become new creatures through the indwelling Holy Spirit.

A caterpillar is Earth-bound and requires great effort to move from point A to point B. Before we are born again, we too are Earth-bound, sin-bound, and require much fleshly effort to do anything of value. In fact, Jesus said, "apart from Me you can do nothing" (John 15:5). We can be very busy doing nothing for Jesus.

Peter had told Jesus he would die for Him. Yet, he soon denied Him. After Peter was filled with the Spirit, he was empowered to both live and die for Jesus. A. B. Simpson, founder of The Christian and Missionary Alliance, states in *The Christ Life*:

> The glory of the Gospel is that it does not teach us to rise, but shows our inability to do anything good of ourselves, and lays us at once in the grave in utter helplessness and nothingness, and then raises us up into new life, born entirely from above and sustained alone from Heavenly sources. The Christian life is not self-improving, but it is wholly supernatural and divine. Now the resurrection cannot come until there has been the death.

For a caterpillar to become a butterfly, it must first die to being a caterpillar. It must enter a tomb-like chrysalis and wait for God to transform it into a butterfly. We too must die to self to be born again and become new re-creations in Christ. To bring us to the end of our old selves, God must often take us through painful dying experiences before we find new life in Him. Then truly we can say, "I have been crucified with Christ; and it is no longer I who live, but Christ lives in me" (Galatians2:20). Life comes out of a dying process. Jesus went to the cross to prepare a place for us in God's presence here and now. "God has given us eternal life, and this life is in His Son. He who has the Son, has the life" (1 John 5:11). Christ died for us, and now He lives for us and in us. Jesus said He is the Way. He is the way to life in the spiritual realm, both now and in the life to come.

You have probably heard the story of the little boy who tried to help the butterfly out of its' chrysalis, thereby killing it. Our self-effort won't set us free. Like the caterpillar, we must wait for God's strength to be made perfect in our weakness (2 Corinthians 12:9). "But if the Spirit of Him who raised Jesus from the dead dwells in you, He . . . will also give life to your mortal bodies through His Spirit who dwells in you" (Romans 8:11).

As the emerging butterfly's wings begin to unfold, its beauty is revealed as its second nature comes forth. As the life of Jesus begins to be clearly visible in our mortal bodies (2 Corinthians4:11) by the fruit of the Spirit, He will be seen as the Way, the Truth, and the Life. This will not be a feeble imitation of Jesus, but the real Jesus coming forth. We receive a new nature: "I will put My Spirit within you and cause you to walk in My statutes" (Ezekiel 36:27). His nature must become second nature to us. A.B. Simpson also states:

> Christ will not only be the death of
> self, and the power to put old self

aside, by His Spirit and grace, but He will be in us the new life of purity and power. He will cleanse us and let us share His life. And there will be such a sense of its being a life that does not belong to you.

After the butterfly comes forth from the chrysalis, it still cannot fly immediately. It must gain new strength. So too, after we are born again, we still need to be sanctified and learn how to walk in the Spirit. Sadly there are too many of us butterflies still living as caterpillars, struggling to live for Jesus instead of allowing Him to live for us and through us. We must be "strengthened with power through His Spirit in the inner man" (Ephesians 3:16). Supernatural!

> *Jesus' nature must become second nature to us.*

Missionary author Norman Grubb writes in *The Law of Faith:*

> The believer, through reckoning himself dead to sin and alive unto God, becomes henceforth just a channel, Christ the Power; just a branch, Christ the Vine; just a vessel, Christ the

Treasure; just a lamp, Christ the Light; just a cup, Christ the Water.

We must exchange our weakness for God's strength. "Yet those who wait for the Lord will gain new strength; they will mount up with wings like eagles" (Isaiah 40:31).

After the butterfly takes wing, it requires little effort to move to where God's breezes take it. What a contrast from life as a caterpillar. Led of the Spirit, we can "mount up with wings like eagles" and with little effort let the breath or Spirit of God take us to places we have never imagined. We can gloriously lose ourselves and rise to new life in Christ. "In Him we live and move and have our being" (Acts 17:28). Christ becomes the very atmosphere in which we live and the air we breathe. We need no longer be driven by the need of the moment, but led by the Spirit of Life.

> *Let God's Spirit take you to places you never imagined.*

Jesus said in John 3:7–8, "Do not be amazed that I said to you, 'You must be born again.' The wind blows where it wishes and you hear the sound of it, but do not know where it comes from and where it is going; so is everyone who is born of the Spirit." The Greek word (pneumos) for wind is the same word for breath or spirit. At creation, God breathed His breath or Spirit into man and he became alive. When man sinned, he died spiritually and was no longer indwelt by the Spirit of God. Jesus died to restore that indwelling Spirit of God in us. "I in them" (John 17:26) was His final prayer in Jesus' final message before the cross.

> *Christ becomes the very atmosphere in which we live and the air we breathe.*

Whatever comes our way, we can rest in the Lord, for He lifts us up above our Earthly cares to clouds of peace and joy. When trials come, we can say with the Apostle Paul, "None of these things move me" (Acts 20:24).

"Therefore if you have been raised up with Christ, keep seeking the things above, where Christ is, seated at the right hand of God. Set your mind on the things above, not on the things that are on the Earth, for you have died and your life is hidden with Christ in God. When Christ, who is our life, is revealed, then you also will be revealed with Him in glory" (Colossians 3:1–4).

Jesus, in introducing the New Covenant, told His disciples the Spirit was with them, but would soon be in them (John 14:17). After Jesus rose from the dead, He breathed on them and said, "Receive the Holy Spirit" (John 20:22). Earlier Jesus had said, "It is the Spirit who gives life; the flesh profits nothing" (John 6:63). Then at Pentecost, the Spirit, or breath of God, swept in like a rushing wind and filled them with His life.

Breathe on us, oh breath of God we pray. Restore a right Spirit within us. Let us yield to the gentle breath of your Spirit to take us where You wish. May Your supernatural indwelling life be clearly seen by those all around us who desperately need You. Then we can say with Jesus who also lived by the life of Another, "I do nothing on My own initiative, but I speak these things as the Father taught Me."

Finally, I pray: "That you may really come to know practically, through experience for yourselves, the love of Christ, which far surpasses mere knowledge without experience; that you may be filled through all your being unto all the fullness of God; may have the richest measure of the divine Presence, and become a body wholly filled and flooded with God Himself . . . To Him be glory in the church and in Christ Jesus throughout all generations forever and ever. Amen" (Ephesians 3:19, 21, Amplified Bible).

Made in the USA
Middletown, DE
22 September 2017